Santorini Escape:

Life, Love, and Travel

A Novel by

Jim LaBuda

Jim LaBuda

COPYRIGHT

Santorini Escape:
Life, Love, and Travel

Copyright © 2016 Jim LaBuda

All rights reserved.

Published in the United States of America

ISBN-13: 978-1530355150
ISBN-10: 153035515X

DEDICATION

This book is dedicated to...

Jim LaBuda

ACKNOWLEDGMENTS

The Island of Santorini is known for its beauty and amazing vistas. Yet, this incredible island finds its way into my heart through its beautiful people and their warm hospitality. My wife and I cherish the time we spend at the Boathouse Hotel in Kamari and with its owners the Zorzos family. They not only have shared their hotel, but their family, friends, and traditions...as well as a few glasses of wine.

This novel would not be possible without the support and input from my beautiful, loving wife, Susan. She is my traveling partner and my partner in life. She is at my side every mile and every day. She inspires me and I am a better person because of her.

Credit also needs to be given to Carolyn "CJ" Sich, my chief editor. Her literary knowledge is incredible. I have always valued her opinion and expertise. She is wise beyond her years.

Editing credit should also be given to Leora Bennett for her commitment and insightful suggestions.

Special thanks to Carol Zimmerman of The von Raesfeld Agency. I am grateful for her guidance and assistance through the publishing process. Her expertise enabled this book to be published.

Thank you to Leora Bennett, Mo Flores, Diane Zorzos and Spyros Zorzos for serving as my focus group.

I appreciated their time and input. They are trusted friends. Special thanks to Diane and Spyros for their insights on Greek culture and traditions.

I appreciated the creative talents and marketing skills of Linda Burns, CLB Global Services, Inc. Her marketing plan provided the tools enabling this book to reach its potential.

I must also acknowledge my own children: Carolyn, Ricky, and Andre. They were an inspiration for writing this novel – more than they will ever understand. They are all young adults venturing off on their own careers. May they learn of the world around them and experience life through traveling. My love will always accompany them.

Map of Santorini

Jim LaBuda

Chapter 1
Port of Santorini

*Life is a journey best navigated with a partner.
Those who travel the path together will share
in life's pleasures, encounter its challenges,
and endure any pain that follows.*

Sara leaned on my shoulder. We both gazed out at the incredible, bird's-eye view from the caldera rim on the island of Santorini. It was breathtaking. Lining the sea, the sunlight illuminated the dark, jagged, volcanic rocks of the sheer cliffs. Reflecting below were the brilliant blues of the sea, which gradually met the sun-bleached hues of the Greek sky. The pallet of calming blues was the background of a heavenly creation that we could look at forever.

The barren, lifeless nature of the cliffside that served as a frame for this majestic picture was softened with sprays of white daisies and patches of purple and yellow wildflowers. Traditional white Greek buildings balanced on the caldera rim. Their foundations clung to the side of the rugged cliffs, each building assembled as if it were supported by the one below it. Though they looked like they might slide into the sea below, these buildings had been clinging to the cliffs for hundreds of years.

One of the most photographed settings in the world, Santorini was created by a volcanic eruption 3,600 years ago. The only lasting evidence of the violent eruption was the severe, jagged wall of the caldera that still outlined where the ancient island had crumbled into the sea. Perched high on the edge of the rim, 400 yards above the Aegean Sea, we could clearly make out the circular remains of the original island sweeping along the caldera and onto the outer islands, which were once part of Santorini prior to the volcanic eruption.

Our eyes focused on the white ribbon of hotels, shops, homes, and churches that ran along the edge of the volcanic crater. Many buildings were highlighted by vivid Greek blue window frames and doors. The churches wore enormous blue domes, making them easy to pick out. Swimming pools provided opalescent dabs of reflected sunlight in between the crowds of white and blue buildings. People made tiny by the distance, moved along the winding walkways and the steep stairs of the village.

It had only been two weeks since we'd retired. Our world, normally defined by routines, seemed to come to a halt. The current quiet moment seemed to give us a glimpse of new opportunities. I watched my wife, relaxed and content, observe the new world around her.

Far below our perch on the caldera was the cruise ship that had brought us to this island. This huge ship, which carried 3,000 passengers, looked very small as it waited silently in the sea hundreds of yards below us. This was a journey that was booked well in advance to celebrate the life-long goal of retirement. Though we had anticipated this moment and dreamed of experiencing Santorini, the beauty that lay in front of us was more than we ever imagined.

My wife gripped my hand and in return, I gripped hers. The light sense of pressure of her hand in mine was reassuring. We'd been married for 35 years, but we often reminded each other of our commitment and love. This was a special time—a special moment—in our lives. I wanted to remember it forever.

The road to retirement was filled with many years of work in the field of education. Sara was a high school art teacher. Herself a thing of beauty, she enjoyed her working years and was a talented painter. I was an elementary school principal, a job that certainly kept me busy. I was known as "Doc" because I'd earned a doctorate in educational administration. Most of my friends called me Jay, which was far from the formal title of Dr. LaFarve.

Our careers never made us wealthy, but certainly provided a comfortable life for our family. We raised three children, all of whom are now young adults. All three graduated from college and ventured on to their own careers. This moment, sitting along the wall overlooking the amazing panoramic view of Santorini's caldera, certainly validated our choice of retirement.

We stared out across the vast sea. Two small islands, Nea (New) Kameni and Palea (Old) Kameni sat outside the harbor as if they were guarding our cruise ship. The black lava likened the surface of the islands to that of the moon. They appeared barren and lifeless.

The tender boats, which shuttle cruise ship passengers, scuttled between shore and the cruise ship looking like ants along a food route. Three boats appeared to serve our ship for the passengers currently returning.

The brilliant hues of color radiated in every direction. The cruise ship, the village, and the tender boats all were a brilliant white. The dark tones of earthy reds, blacks, and browns revealed the rugged aspect of the land. Greens and yellows were limited, but provided reminders of early summer growth. Blues, literally every shade imaginable, speckled the village and then spilled out into the ocean and sky.

Though little was said between us, there was no doubt that both of us were enjoying just sitting along the wall and soaking in all that was in front of us. Greece had always been on our bucket list, but the expense of traveling halfway around the world and the responsibilities of raising a family had put that desire out of reach. In fact, until this trip, most of our travel was limited to long weekends, family outings, and an annual trip back to the Midwest to visit relatives. All these ventures were enjoyable, but we yearned for more adventurous travel for extended periods of time.

We had flown to Athens, Greece only seven days earlier. The eleven-hour flight was spent sipping wine, nibbling airline munchies, and dreaming together of the travel ahead. It was our first time visiting Europe. The anticipation heightened the closer we came to the historical city.

Once there, we found ourselves in a small boutique hotel: *Fresh*. It was a bit on the outskirts of the Plaka, but close enough to walk to many of the historical sites. It was also a convenient location to catch the green line metro to Piraeus, the cruise ship port south of Athens.

With only one day of sightseeing before the cruise, we fended off jet lag and the slight wine headaches. We hopped on the Red Bus to enjoy a quick tour of Athens and its incredible landmarks, but we still felt the anticipation building for our real desire, which was to experience the islands of Greece.

That evening, sitting on the roof deck of our hotel, we had a beautiful view of the Parthenon. It's perched on a hill overlooking Athens, with soft lights focused on its majestic columns. The moon and stars highlighted the ancient site from above. It was a magical, peaceful evening. We sipped wine, talking in anticipation of the cruise and our time on the islands.

As we sat on the caldera nearly a week later, our cruise was nearly over. We'd stopped in Mykonos, Patmos, Rhodes, and now Santorini. *The Norwegian Jade* was a marvelous ship. The grand foyer and the elegant dining certainly made us feel as if retirement was treating us well.

Our only disappointment was not in the beauty of the islands, nor the service provided by the ship, but the limited time we were in each port. Our stop at each island, the destinations we had researched and dreamed about, was only four to six hours per port—long enough to say we'd been there, but much too short to explore the culture and experience daily life in the area. That left the majority of our time to enjoy the pleasures of the ship; however, we both yearned for more time on the islands.

We were trying to enjoy every last second of the time we had from our majestic perch on the caldera rim. An occasional glance at my watch indicated that our 4:00 p.m. departure time was drawing near. With our ship docked in the harbor, we would need to find our way through the winding streets of Fira to the cable car. The five minute descent in the car would take us to the pier that we could see far below us. Then we would have to allow enough time to take the tender boat from the pier to our ship. The time was not a thing to ignore as cruise ships tend to keep their schedule and leave passengers behind.

A quick glance at my watch indicated the time was nearly 3:00 p.m. and the inevitable words came out of my mouth: "We'd better head back to the ship."

Sara glanced up at me. Her deep blue eyes looked directly into my eyes. She settled back down and nuzzled her head under my chin. "Not yet."

"You don't really want to go, do you?" I knew full well that she could spend the rest of the day in the same spot.

"No, Jay, I really don't."

"How long do you want to stay?"

"Forever," her voice had no hesitation.

I didn't move and I didn't respond. I wanted her to enjoy every second available to her. I did sneak a peek at my watch, only to confirm that we had very few precious minutes left; however, I gave no indication that we needed to leave.

There was a full minute of silence. I don't think either of us moved a muscle. We stared off into an endless panoramic view, enjoying it as much as we had the first moment we laid eyes on it. The vast sea sparkled in the sunlight. The black volcanic cliffs seemed to curve along the sea forever. The colors in every direction were vivid. The blue domes of the Greek Churches stood proudly throughout the villages. The view was awe-inspiring, as well as peaceful and calming.

As the seconds ticked away, the silence was beginning to create an uneasy feeling in my stomach and I was sure Sara felt the same churning inside.

I broke the silence. "Forever?"

"Forever."

I could only respond with a small chuckle and a gentle hug. We sat there in silence for another thirty seconds, an endless amount of time when you're hoping the other would break the silence and say something.

Then Sara spoke, probably the most sincere words I'd ever heard her speak. "I really don't want to leave."

The same little laugh that slipped from my mouth earlier again seemed to be my first reaction. I took a deep breath and replied, "I know you don't want to leave, but if we don't go now, we'll miss the ship."

She responded with the same conviction. "I really don't want to leave. I want to stay."

"You want to let the ship sail away with our clothes, passports, and all the souvenirs you bought?"

Sara responded quickly, as if she'd already thought this through. "We can go back to the ship, grab our belongings, and notify the crew that we are leaving."

"Are you serious? Then what?" I glanced again at my watch.

"We return to this spot and start enjoying this Greek island the way we dreamed we would." Sara stared into my eyes. I knew from the intensity of the look that she was serious.

As precious time ticked away, I moved from my rigid, hunched position and sat more upright. I reached over and put my hands squarely on Sara's shoulders. I looked straight into her focused blue eyes and answered, "Whether we stay or return, we need to go

7

back to the ship now. We can discuss this in more detail on the cable car down to the port."

She responded instantly, "I want a commitment now. Tell me you'll stay with me. Jay, I want to do this!"

My mind was racing. I was the detail person. I was the planner. I thought about procedures for leaving the ship, changing flights, our house, and seemingly a million other things, but I knew Sara was serious. This was her dream. Our dream. My hands now held both of her hands. I gripped them firmly. My eyes saw nothing but her eyes. She was the total focus of my existence. The panoramic view with the tiny ship far below had somehow disappeared. I knew I needed to respond.

"This is crazy!" I barked.

"Spontaneous!" she championed and added, "This is something we've always wanted to do and this is our chance. We've got to take it."

I knew she was right, but it was still crazy. She hadn't made any attempt to stand, let alone head toward the ship. She wanted to seize this opportunity and her intentions were perfectly clear. Though I knew it was crazy, there was an urge inside of me to agree with her and leave the ship. We were retired, our kids were on their own, and I couldn't come up with any reasons not to agree.

I grinned. I had a beautiful woman in front of me urging me to make a spontaneous, though perhaps somewhat irrational decision. With my grin widening and my head shaking sideways, I replied, "This is the craziest thing I have ever—" I stopped and shut my eyes. I took a deep breath. "Let's do it."

She smiled and suddenly lunged towards me. "Really?"

"Really. It'll be an adventure."

We embraced each other so tight I could feel her heartbeat. We held that embrace for a few seconds and as we released each other, our eyes connected again. She had tears in her eyes. There was no turning back. Without a word, we jumped to our feet and headed down the walkway along the caldera wall in search of the cable car. Our hands gripped each other tightly.

Chapter 2
Returning to the Ship

The degree of satisfaction in life is a direct result of our choices. We are empowered to define our path in life. Positive choices can alter and strengthen our lives forever.

The cable car departed from the village of Fira, Santorini's port city which sat at the top of the caldera. It descended to Skala—the old port where the cruise ships docked. The small cable car, filled to capacity with two other couples, didn't provide an opportunity for much private talk. Our fellow travelers seemed to be more interested in taking pictures of the ship in the water below than striking up a conversation. That was totally fine with us as our thoughts were focused on leaving the ship. The five-minute descent was filled with mischievous glances at each other, some acknowledging smiles, and a few school-kid giggles as we kept the secret of our "escape plan."

The humming of the cable car engine and grinding of the steel cables left me in thought. My head seemed to bob with the motion of the car, but I was wondering if I wasn't actually shaking it in disbelief. We were leaving the cruise ship early. This quick decision by Sara was really out of character. Yes, she could insist on getting something she wanted, but she was normally easygoing and willing to accept things for what they were. She might express her desire to stay longer on the islands, but to insist on leaving with no plans in place—it was totally out of character.

I glanced at my wife. She smiled in return, pressing her lips together as if our secret plan was trying to burst out. There was no sign of regret or hesitation – she was set on escaping to Santorini. I had an electric feeling running through my veins that numbed my fingertips – a strange mix of nerves and adventure. I marveled at Sara's determination and willingness to jump into this adventure.

As we exited the packed cable car, we immediately hustled to the line for the waiting tender boats which were shuttling passengers back to the ship. The maze wove back and forth in front of us. We were able to walk through most of the maze until we were finally halted by the line of fellow passengers. Waiting the anticipated fifteen minutes in line was really the first chance Sara and I had to speak.

When Sara spoke, her voice was an almost inaudible whisper. "I'll pack our backpacks."

I'd put my administrator mind into gear during the cable car descent. I was mapping out the procedures and steps to our disembarkation. There were several issues that needed to be addressed. The first issue that came to mind was the time factor. I glanced back and the maze appeared to be filling in with more passengers. I hoped that their rides to the ship on the tender boats would provide us with some additional time to get back to shore. I anticipated we'd have about thirty minutes on the ship and then we'd be able to catch one of the last tender boats going back to Santorini. The details churned through my head.

"Sara, we'll need to notify the ship."

"You take care of that while I'm packing."

"I will, but I need to think this through. What if they don't let us off?"

Her eyes grew wide in disbelief. "Not let us off?"

"It's a possibility." I remembered a co-worker talking about a cruise he took from Long Beach to Mexico. He'd had a business engagement come up and had wanted to get off at the ship's first stop, but the captain informed him that it was not a possibility because the ship had not visited a foreign port. I didn't remember all the details, but I knew this applied to ships sailing from the U.S. and they didn't let him off. I hoped this wouldn't be an issue for us, but it was a concern that rolled around in the back of my mind. "I'll write a note to the Captain and give it to the Purser. By the time you're done packing the bags, we should be ready."

"Is he the right person?"

"I think so, he's the officer who handles money and lots of the day-to-day operations. There's a Purser's desk in the main lobby. If he's not there, someone else from the staff will be."

"How much time do you think we have?"

My mind was racing. "I'd say we have 15-20 minutes in the room—max. If we take any longer, they won't let us take a tender boat back to the port."

By now we were at the head of the line to return to the ship. We found ourselves being assisted by a crew member into the tender boat. We moved forward and took our seats in the middle of the boat. The other twenty passengers on board chatted and displayed the souvenirs they'd bought on Santorini. While they shared and waved white Greek cotton clothing and laughed at donkey imprinted t-shirts, we planned our departure as the boat moved away from the volcanic walls and towards the ship.

I whispered to Sara, "When we dock at the ship, we'll both run to the room. I'll write the letter to the Captain and you pack. Just jam the stuff in our backpacks."

"Don't you think we should tell them in person that we're leaving?" Sara asked.

"No! What if they say no?" I took a breath, held it for a moment, and then let the air escape through my teeth. "If we're really doing this, we just need to do it."

Sara reached out and pressed her hand into mine. "Then a note it is. I'm with you."

As the tender boat pulled up to the ship, we leaned to the center and inched toward the front. Truthfully, our fellow passengers probably thought we were rude, but they didn't know we were on a mission. As the onboard crew secured the boat to the side of the ship with bulky, weathered rope, Sara was the first passenger to extend her hand to the assisting crew member. He guided her as she stepped safely from the bobbing tender boat. I stood immediately behind her and quickly exited the small craft.

We glanced at each other with determined looks and a quick smile. Her smile crinkled the corners of her eyes; she seemed almost playful. My nerves were turning my arms to rubber. I knew that we had challenges in getting off the ship, not to mention we hadn't even begun to discuss what we were going to do once we returned to Santorini.

We moved toward the checkpoint within the ship's hull and scanned our cruise cards. This was a regular formality that we'd done at each port. Cruise ships have high security and verify the identification of each passenger returning to the ship. Since we had the proper cards, which were given to us upon arrival our first day, we passed through the checkpoint quickly. We raced up the steps on our way to the room.

Our feet made urgent beats up the stairs. This spontaneous decision had definitely changed the purpose of our day and had thrown us into a hurried chaos. I thought back to the motionless state we were in as we sat mesmerized by the view from the caldera. It seemed like a lifetime ago. Without speaking, Sara and I moved in tandem up the stairs until we reached the fifth deck, made a sharp left turn and headed to our room, 5034.

I reached for my key card. It seemed to be caught on the corners of my pocket, but in reality, I think it was my hands shaking in my hurried attempt to get the key. I fumbled with the key and finally popped the door open. Sara quickly slipped in between the door and the wall, squeezing into the room. There was barely enough room for her slender body to pass. By the time I put my key in my pocket and turned to enter the room, she had a backpack in her hand and was moving towards the small dresser top in the cabin. In one swipe half the make-up and brushes, which were on the dresser top, were sliding into the bottom of the backpack.

It was a good thing we'd decided to travel light. We had each brought one standard carry-on that converted into a backpack. They were large enough to fit our essentials and small enough to meet the carry-on size restrictions of Aegean Airlines, which we flew to Athens. Most European airlines only allow "hold luggage" that is slightly smaller in size than U.S. airline carry-on guidelines and have weight limits of approximately twenty pounds. These lighter, smaller pieces of luggage may have made our packing challenging, but they certainly were an asset in our preparation to escape to the island.

As Sara continued her frantic packing pace, I scrambled through the nightstand drawer to find a pen and a pad. I grabbed the daily program for the ship. I scanned the schedule and the related information. My eyes finally fixated on what I was searching for. Right in the middle of the front page was an invitation to the Captain's Dinner. Captain George Kostopoulos was inviting all the guests to join him for a welcome cocktail and dinner in the ship's formal dining room. *Well, finally a free drink on the ship and we were leaving,* I humorously thought to myself. I had more than one $8 glass of wine during the last week.

I took a deep breath and carefully scripted a greeting for the Captain, "Dear Capt. Kostopoulos." I paused briefly to gather my thoughts. "I, Jay LaFarve, and my wife, Sara, have decided to leave the ship. We enjoyed our cruise, but would like to spend more time on Santorini." My hand was sweaty and trembling, but I continued to write. "We have removed our personal items from our cabin, #5034. Please accept our apologies for our early departure."

I signed the note and started to seal the envelope that was left for the steward's tip. Noticing the steward's name on the envelope, I quickly pulled out my wallet and included a few twenties before sealing it. I completed the task by writing the Captain's name on the front of the envelope.

With the note completed and sealed, I turned and sprinted towards the door, yelling to Sara, "I'm taking the note to the Purser. I'll be right back."

I heard fading words of encouragement from Sara as I ran down the hallway. "Go for it!"

I side-stepped an older couple at the base of the stairs and took the next three steps in one leap, not caring about manners or politeness. I made my way to the seventh floor of the ship, which was the main lobby and the location of the Purser's desk. The purser was assisting an older woman who appeared to have some issues with her room credit. Ships always seem to have confusing credit deals if you book in advance or as part of a special promotion. This is the type of conversation and topic that would normally interest me, but I was preoccupied with getting off the ship as quickly as possible.

Again I set my manners aside and held the envelope in front of the Purser's nose. Trying not to breathe too heavily or look in need of oxygen, I asked, "Could you please forward this to the Captain as soon as possible?"

He looked puzzled and annoyed that he'd been interrupted from the conversation with the elderly passenger. His half-hearted response, "Ah – yes, Sir," was good enough for me.

I walked briskly away from the Purser's desk in the direction of the stairs. I was restraining every urge to immediately sprint, though my pace quickened down the staircase.

As I flung the door to our room open, huffing and puffing, I saw Sara jamming the last of my clothing into my backpack. As she pushed down on the clothing and pulled the zipper shut, she yelled, "Done! Phone, keys, wallets, passports...done!"

I complimented her with a resounding "Great!" and then pulled her towards me for one reassuring hug. This embrace rivaled the embrace on the caldera. We were in this together.

We made one last sweep of the room looking for any belongings that may have been left behind. I reaffirmed Sara's work by saying, "Looks like you have everything."

She paused, took one deep breath, and glanced back at the room. "I guess there's a reason we travel light, but who knew this would be it?"

We exited the room. I slung my backpack over my shoulder and started down the hallway. As she usually did, Sara wheeled her pack behind me. Our pace was quick. I glanced over my shoulder to ensure that Sara was still behind me. I got a nod of acknowledgment from her. She was keeping pace.

We both laughed and again she looked playful. It reminded me of our early dating days and the games we played getting to know each other. It was kind of the same look she had in her eyes when we made love for the first time. As we dashed down the halls to complete our mad scheme, I was thinking to myself that we had kept that playfulness and commitment between us over the thirty-five years that we'd been married and raised our three children. Maybe that's why we both were so committed to this crazy plan. It wasn't that we were comfortable with leaving the ship, nor were we sure what we were going to do after we left the ship, but we knew we were doing it together – and that seemed to be the unifying force behind our plan.

As we reached the staircase, we needed to descend four flights to the area where we would disembark the ship. As if it had been thoroughly rehearsed, I turned at the top of the stairs and grabbed the handle on Sara's pack. She let go, swung past me, and quickly darted down the stairs. There was a slight thump when she hit the first landing and made her turn to descend further. Like in many airports and hotels from our family travel, I was well-versed in carrying her things. I knew as soon as I hit the bottom step Sara would be there waiting for her pack and ready to proceed to the disembarking area.

I jumped off the last step, handing off Sara's pack in effortless fashion. We both scampered up to the two crew members who were greeting other passengers as they boarded the ship from the tender boats. One was a stern-looking older man in what appeared to be an officer's uniform. The other crew member was a middle-aged woman in a nautical uniform, but not as decorated as her partner.

We were like salmon swimming upstream, as all other passengers were arriving to the checkpoint from port and returning to their rooms. There was an odd pause as we approached the checkpoint. The two crew members were focused on the incoming passengers. We waited for them to finish checking in a family.

They started to assist the next couple coming in behind the family; however, I jumped into their view. "Excuse me, we'd like to take a tender boat into the port for a few more minutes."

The stern man who appeared to be in charge, responded quickly and abruptly, "We just stopped the trips to shore. We are only bringing passengers on board." My heart seemed to skip a beat and my stomach churned. The next second seemed endless and I couldn't get any words out of my throat.

Then Sara's voice pierced the silence and responded to the crew member. "We need to go back. I left my wedding ring in the bathroom by the passenger loading maze." That hardly drew the attention of the male crew member, but her words were accompanied by fresh tears and an agonizing wail. The female crew member then reached out and put her hand on Sara's shoulder. I also put my arm around her to show that I also understood her pain.

The uniformed woman looked over at the man, who shook his head in disbelief – or possibly disapproval, but he gestured to us to move forward to the tender boat. The female crew member then accompanied us to the tender boat and gave her approval for us to be transported back to Santorini. We slid into the tender boat with the three men who staffed the vessel. I held my wife in a comforting fashion, assuring her that we'd find the ring in the bathroom.

As we watched the small boat move away from the ship, we once again found ourselves in a reassuring embrace. With my right hand wrapped around her shoulder, I reached with my left hand and grasped her left hand. I then realized that Sara had slipped off her wedding ring. My spontaneous, creative partner had acted quickly in a critical moment of the great escape and we were successfully on our way back to Santorini.

Chapter 3
Safely in Fira

*Dreams can turn into reality if we are willing to
pursue them. Some people dream of tomorrow.
Others act on their dreams today.*

The tender boat rumbled towards shore and the steep
walls of jagged rock that guarded Santorini. We craned
our necks to see the white-washed buildings of Fira that
coated the top of the dark cliffs. This natural barrier
stood between us and our dreams.

The water rolled symmetrically from the sides of the
boat, as we made our way towards the port. Glancing
back, the widening wake framed our deserted ship in
the background. We were steadily moving farther from
the massive vessel and closer to the island port.

We leaned on each other as I continued to show
support for Sara and her mythical lost wedding ring.
She would rub her eyes intermittently throughout our
short voyage and add a few sympathetic sniffles for
character. Our acting skills seemed to be convincing
enough as the three bored crew members on board
showed little concern for us. It seemed that our return
voyage was no different than the many they had run
back and forth all day. Though I was surprised that no
one seemed to question why we had our backpacks. I
smiled, giving Sara's acting skills credit for the
successful departure.

We stayed in character throughout the ten minute ride. A few consoling remarks were exchanged between Sara and me, as well as a few reassuring embraces. The words about the lost ring just fell off our lips with no purpose other than to fill time and remain convincing to the young crew members. The embraces were genuine, as I needed reassurance that we were making the right decision.

Many thoughts were still snaking through my brain. *What if the Purser had delivered the message to the captain and he ordered us to be detained when we disembarked at the port? What if the two crew members at the ship's security check point had radioed ahead to the port instructing them to make sure we boarded one of the remaining tender boats and return to the ship? What would happen if they were concerned for our safety and started searching for us?* Our goal to leave the ship was within reach but there were some possible complications.

Through all this concern, I marveled at how quickly and effectively Sara had stepped in to save our opportunity to leave the ship. I reflected back to the determined look in her eyes as she turned towards me on top of the caldera and told me she wanted to stay on the island. While I continued to worry about potential problems at the port area, somewhere in the back of my mind I also started to wonder about Sara's desperate need to stay on the island.

The slowing tender boat pulled up to the port dock. It bumped the pier with a thud and it nearly jarred us to the floor. Perhaps we were in too much of a hurry to exit, as we were nearly on our feet when the boat rammed the pier. We stumbled toward the exit.

The crew members waiting there glanced at us curiously, since they had not expected incoming passengers. They grabbed the thick, water-logged ropes attached to the tender boat and quickly secured them to the concrete pylons along the pier. I saw a crew member from the boat give an approving nod to the crew port side and we were assisted out of the docked boat. Sara sniffled and wiped her eyes as the crew member released her hand. I again reassured her and saying loud enough for others in the vicinity to hear, "We'll find your wedding ring, Honey. I'm sure you left it there." There were a few looks of concern from waiting passengers as they overheard my comment and saw Sara's reddened eyes; however, most just appeared eager for their turn to board the waiting tender boat and return to their comfy staterooms on the ship.

We headed toward the rustic bathrooms, which were about 100 yards from the loading maze. This gave us some separation from the other passengers and a chance to communicate with each other.

Sara continued walking towards the restrooms and asked, "Now what?"

"Go in the bathroom for a minute and pretend to look for your ring. I'll figure out what's going on out here—if anyone's looking for us."

Sara quickly moved towards the women's bathroom door, adding another sniffle for effect. Feeling like I was on a reconnaissance mission, I glanced over at the maze queuing the passengers returning to the ship. There were approximately thirty people in line. The tender boat we just exited was quickly loading passengers and another was approaching from about 200 yards out.

The second tender would definitely be able to transport the remaining passengers. We had maybe twenty minutes until all passengers were situated on the small boats and another ten to fifteen minutes for the last tender to return to the ship. Then it would be only a matter of time until the ship's security checkpoint would review the passenger count and realize that our ship identification cards were not scanned on return.

When we first arrived in the Old Port of Santorini early that morning, the tour guides had informed us that there were three ways to the top of the caldera where the village of Fira was located. The first option was a donkey ride, at a cost of eight euros per person, on a narrow trail weaving back and forth up the volcanic wall. The trip on the overburdened animals would take approximately forty-five minutes. The second option was walking the same trail with our own legs at no cost. Assuming we could keep up with the tired donkeys, it would still take us forty-five minutes. The third option was returning to the top via a five-minute cable-car ride for five euros, as we had done previously. There was no doubt I wanted to escape via the cable car.

Sara cautiously peeked out through the crack of the weathered door of the women's bathroom. I motioned by slightly moving my head in one direction for her to come. I then grabbed her hand and led her away. My directions slipped out in a hurried whisper, even though we were far enough from the lines that no one would overhear us.

"Let's get on the cable car quickly. It'll only be about thirty minutes before they realize that we haven't returned to the ship."

Sara was quick to add, "They may know already if the Purser gave your note to the Captain."

"You're right and who knows—they may not even care. We did let them know that weren't returning."

We both ran up to the empty loading area for the cable car. There were no other passengers going up to Fira and only a few hurried ship passengers making their way down from the village to the ship.

As we boarded the empty car, I watched two passengers run at a good clip to the tender boat loading maze. They were slightly overweight and carrying an array of sacks and packages.

"You know if they miss the last tender boat the ship will leave them." I laughed at how frantically they were trying to get back to the boat at the same time we were frantically trying to escape it.

Sara laughed too. "Then why do I feel like we're breaking out of prison?"

"If we are, we're escaping from a five-star prison which we paid good money to be in, a prison with great food and comfy beds."

Sara's tone changed a bit. She turned those steel blue eyes towards me with an intense look on her face. "I really want to do this, Jay. No concerns about money, no worries about consequences, and no worries about details. I want to do this." The intensity I'd heard earlier was back in her voice.

I stopped laughing and looked at her seriously. "I'm your partner in crime and this is part of our dream. Besides, it's too late to turn back now."

She grabbed my hand and held it in her lap. Outside the car window, the ship was still sitting in the harbor and appeared smaller the higher we moved toward the top of the caldera rim. I stared down at the shrinking ship. "No turning back now."

We had a few more minutes to conclude our ride in the cable car. I was feeling a little more at ease because I realized that the five-hour time limit that was in place on the ship's itinerary was now lifted. I wanted to get out and explore the island. I started paying attention to the coastline and the natural beauty beyond the caldera.

I turned toward Sara. "No more five-hour time limit."

"Nope. I was thinking the same thing." She smiled as she looked out the car window. "I know I should feel nervous, but I am feeling more relaxed."

"Me too. Enjoy it. We'll figure out the details."

"I am. It's perfect."

I thought about the fact that cruise ships leave late passengers. They knew we were off the ship because of the note and our ID cards. They shouldn't be worried about anything, at least nothing that I could foresee. I certainly hoped that our leaving the ship didn't delay the departure for the rest of the passengers.

Sara leaned against the wall of the cable car and watched as we approached the village of Fira. She wasn't looking back at the ship. Her vision and thoughts seemed to be focused on our destination.

"What would you like to do first in Fira?" I asked.

"Have a glass of wine!

I laughed. She smiled and squeezed my hand. I suddenly had a thought. "Oh, shit!" I thumped my forehead with the palm of my hand.

"What's wrong?" The tension in her voice was palpable.

"Wine! I forgot to pay the bar bill on the ship!"

Sara laughed and jokingly slapped my shoulder. "Don't scare me like that!"

I looked at her and couldn't help but laugh too. "In all the hurry to leave, I never once thought about our bar bill, but I did tip the cabin steward. Damn! They'll probably start a manhunt for me now."

"What do you think they'll do?"

"I'm sure I'll get a bill. If not, I'll contact them when we get home."

"I guess we aren't done dealing with the ship." Sara wiped her eyes. They teared up whenever she laughed too hard.

The cable car was halting as we arrived at the top. It slowed, but continued to move. The door was opened by a smiling attendant. Sara and I exited. We both took deep breaths as we moved away from the cable car. It was like we'd left all our worries behind us. My muscles started to relax for the first time in a couple of hours. Our pace was slow and methodical. We'd made it. We actually completed our escape.

As we strolled out of the cable car area, my eyes scanned the numerous restaurants that lined the caldera. A large portion of the crowd had dwindled since the cruise ship passengers left. There was more room to negotiate the streets. The whole village had a calmer feeling. The tourists that had crowded the streets and formed long lines at the shops had scurried away.

The restaurants all appeared to have a beautiful, uninterrupted view over the harbor. The sun had shifted more to the west and the sea waters had turned to a dark, inky blue. A few steps ahead, a cheerful restaurant owner motioned for us to join him on the second floor of the next building. Because we are both tall and blond, he smiled and called to us in German. It was a common mistake on this trip. I laughed and responded, "U.S.A."

He quickly changed his tone and language. "Oh Americans. Let me take care of you! We have good Santorini wine."

Sara looked at me and nodded. We were both looking forward to a chilled glass of locally grown white wine.

We made our way up the two steep flights of stairs to the *Caldera View* restaurant. The owner, a friendly Greek, exhibited the much appreciated Greek hospitality and welcomed us to his restaurant. The yellow chairs and tablecloths of the charming space provided the welcome we were seeking. He pulled a chair out for Sara at a small, clean table with a perfect view of the harbor. I sat beside her. I ordered two glasses of Gaia wine, which was a renowned winery on Santorini. The island wine industry had made great strides in recent years and the quality of the wine was being recognized around the world. I had done my research.

As the restaurant owner left to retrieve our wine, I couldn't help noticing our cruise ship in the depths of the harbor. It looked like a small boat in a bathtub from 400 yards above. I could see what looked like the last tiny, tender boat arriving at the base of the ship. "I hope that last couple we saw dashing from the cable car made it aboard."

Sara giggled. "We could have traveling companions."

"As soon as the last people get off that tender and walk through the security station, they'll have to decide if they'll leave us."

"The captain may have already read the note." She rolled her eyes. "As my mother would say, 'we just need to let the universe deal with it.'"

We joked about the New Age philosophy of some of her family members; however, in this case, leaving things to the universe was probably the best course of action. We needed to toss out our concerns and let the ship deal with our absence.

The restaurant owner arrived with the chilled wine. He'd promised that he'd take care of us and now he personally delivered our wine to our table, instead of one of his waiters.

"*Yamas*," he said as he set the glasses in front of us.

"*Yamas*," we replied, the Greek equivalent to "Cheers" in English. We clinked our glasses and took our first sip of wine.

As we both set our glasses on the table, we glanced up and noticed our ship was moving steadily across the calm, blue sea, heading out of port.

Sara held up her glass for another toast. "There she goes!" Again, we clinked our glasses together and took another sip.

"So, what do you want to do sweetie?" I asked.

"Spend my life exploring the world with you," she replied. She sounded so certain.

"Wow! That's commitment," I chuckled. "But I'm thinking more about what you want to do, say in the next 24 hours—or what you want to do tonight?"

"You're such a realist," she sighed.

"If a realist is someone who wants to find a place to sleep tonight, yes." I sipped my wine and waited to hear what her plans were. That sense of concern started to coil around my brain again. *How long would we stay? Where would we stay? Did we need to rent a car?*

"Let's just get a place in Fira tonight and enjoy the view," she recommended.

"The hotels on the caldera are very expensive; I'm not sure what type of view we will get."

She shrugged. "I don't need a fancy place and it doesn't have to have a view from our room. We can sit here all night for all I care. I just need a place to sleep."

"If you sat here all night drinking wine, your view would be of the underside of this table."

"Ha, ha, very funny. Let's just keep it simple. We'll finish our wine and then figure out where we should stay."

The restaurant owner returned to our table. He asked if we were enjoying the view.

"It's stunning and very beautiful," said Sara.

I nodded in agreement. "Do you know of any small hotels in the area?"

He quickly acknowledged he did know of a small hotel and boasted of its rooms and location near the bus stop. It wasn't on the caldera where we would enjoy a panoramic view, but it wasn't far from this restaurant. We asked for directions, but he made it clear that he'd call the hotel owner for us. He left our table and headed toward the kitchen.

"What do you think?" I asked Sara.

"It should be fine. We can always take a look at the room before we pay. I'm not looking for a four or five-star hotel. We may be here for a couple of weeks and I don't want to spend all our money at once."

"A couple of weeks!" I responded with alarm.

Sara gave me a mischievous grin. "Well, at least a week."

Just then the restaurant owner returned with two glasses of wine. The look on our faces must have indicated our surprise since we hadn't ordered another glass. The owner smiled. "The owner of the *Stavros Hotel* will be here very soon. Enjoy complimentary wine while you wait."

Now my favorite wines were white and Sara usually selected reds, but the best wines were always complimentary. Using our extremely limited Greek language skills, we responded "*Efharisto*" which allowed us to thank him in Greek.

Once again we clinked our glasses. "*Yamas!*"

The tension was definitely drifting away. I could see Sara scanning the view. For her, this was how a Greek Island should be enjoyed. There was no schedule, nor were there any concerns about getting back to the ship. Here she was, sitting on a Greek island with a glass of local wine. She stared out over the caldera at the blue sea below. "It's like all the pictures in the brochures, only life size—actually more than life size. Larger than life."

"I agree. I never imagined the awe of this view. As beautiful as all the pictures are, I think you have to see it for yourself."

Sara nodded as she scanned the houses along the steep cliffs. She settled back into her chair and adjusted her legs in a more relaxed position. "It's so beautiful that it's almost frightening. Think about it: this used to be a volcano. All this beauty caused by so much destruction...and you're right about the pictures," she added. "You'll never capture it, so just enjoy it." She continued to silently scan the horizon.

I hated to break the silence, but we needed to talk more about our plans. Two hours earlier we were sitting along the caldera wall when Sara turned to me and let me know that she didn't want to return to the ship. That intense look and her focused eyes were etched into my mind. The time since then seemed a blur. But we'd done it—we jumped ship and it left port on schedule at 6:00 p.m. We were in Fira on the beautiful island of Santorini. No going back now.

I decided we needed to discuss our immediate plans. The realist in me couldn't wait any longer. "The hotel owner should be here in a few minutes. How many nights do you think we should book?" I tried to keep my voice light so as not to seem pushy, but I could hear the anxiety in my voice.

Sara pondered for a moment. "How about two nights? That'll give us time to settle in and map out our stay."

"You mean a plan?"

She laughed. "Yes, a plan...just for you. I don't want you to spend our dream vacation worrying. I'm not sure how long we'll stay here, but I think two days will give us a start. I don't really know what there is to do here. Two days for now, more if we need them. What do you say?"

"That's a start. At least it gives me a timeframe to work with. Let's take a look at the room and if it looks fine we can do two nights. I'm sure there's a bunch of things to do in Fira. It's the largest town on the island and it looked like there were plenty of restaurants and shops."

As we waited for the hotel owner to show up, I started thinking about finances and changing our return ticket. I also ran through our home schedule in my mind to see if there was anything we were going to miss because we extended our trip. I couldn't recall any schedule issues—a definite benefit of being retired. I knew the airlines might penalize us a few hundred dollars for changing our flights, but for an additional week or so in Greece and a chance for Sara to live her dream, it was well worth it.

After thinking things through, I told Sara, "I think we're good on our home schedule. I don't think we have any commitments coming up."

"Good. We have Tommy checking the house. He can get the mail. The carrier is going to resume delivery in a couple of days."

Sara had asked our son Tommy to check on the house while we were gone. I knew there was no issue with our house and Tommy would get the mail each day. I also knew he was spending more time in our house than Sara realized, but I didn't want to bother her with the details.

It had only been a short time since the restaurant owner contacted the hotel; however, standing next to our table was a short, dark-haired man holding a photo book—the hotel owner. He introduced himself as Joseph and approached us with a greeting that seemed part welcoming and part sales pitch.

"Welcome to Greece. I have a lovely family hotel for you very close to here. The *Stavros Hotel* has a room you will like, I know it. Only 75 euros a night. Available tonight, right now."

We greeted him, telling him that we appreciated his coming to our current location, not to mention that we were treated to a glass of wine while we waited.

The book contained pictures of the hotel. He proudly flipped through the pages with us, specifically showing us a room that was available. The room and the others in the book were very plain and contained little decorations. We were warned by friends that Greek hotel rooms were usually very modest. They tended to be small, with bare walls and the beds had only thin, firm mattresses.

This room wasn't fancy, but the price was only 75 euros and it was available now. We didn't hesitate to accept Joseph's offer and told him that we would stay in his hotel for two nights. We left a tip for the restaurant owner and followed a smiling Joseph to the *Stavros Hotel*, the first stop in our Santorini adventure.

Chapter 4
Plain and Simple

The simple things in life offer extraordinary opportunities. The secret to a happy life is recognizing opportunities and taking the time to enjoy them.

We wound our way through the narrow, stone covered streets of Fira. They were not as crowded as they were earlier in the day when thousands of passengers from our cruise ship were roaming around. In fact, there was a calm, end-of-the day feeling in the air.

We followed Joseph along the waist high stone wall on the edge of the caldera. The rough molten rock provided a secure, albeit primitive, safety feature. The network of walkways drew my eyes up and down the side of the caldera. There were many secluded patios, restaurants, and pools embedded into the island wall. The late afternoon sun was moving across the sky and its rays splashed across the water. The white buildings along the edge caught the sun, but shadows were now stretching between the roofs. This ancient village was falling asleep.

As we walked, my thoughts drifted back to our time on the cruise. Even though we'd been in such a rush to escape, we did have a great time while we were on board. Each morning we'd get off the ship and explore a new island and each evening we'd have a four-course meal followed by performances in the theater. Sara had looked stunning when she dressed up for the evening shows, even though packing light had limited her to two dresses. She used scarves and accessories to create different looks. Sara adapted like a chameleon to her environment. She looked as comfortable in an evening gown as she did in a flannel shirt and jeans. I had no doubt she'd transition easily from the cruise pampering to the laid back island life of Santorini.

Soon Joseph turned inward and we cut through a side street lined with shops. They were packed from ceiling to floor with souvenirs and local products catering to the thousands of tourists who passed by each day. The shop owners mingled in front of their stores, greeting each passer-by. Joseph did not pause to talk to them, though he nodded as if he knew each one. We were pleased that he kept moving in the direction of his hotel.

Sara walked briskly behind Joseph. Her tall, thin frame contrasted with his stout stature. I thought back to meeting Sara in college. She was a lanky, straight-haired, art student who I would regularly see on her way to class. She would strut through the main courtyard wearing a full length, army-green coat and toting the large, traditional, rust colored portfolio that contained her current drawings. She usually wore glasses, which to me gave her that sexy librarian look. To most others, she probably looked more like an artistic hippy.

Suddenly we stopped. In less than ten minutes we had arrived at the hotel. The outward appearance was more than a bit rustic. It was a rectangular, weathered, white, three-story building. Its doors and window frames were a dark, traditional blue, but the paint was cracked and peeling. A glance at Sara indicated that there might be some concern about our selection of accommodations. We exchanged concerned expressions and continued following Joseph.

He grabbed a ring of keys from his pants pocket and told us that we would have his best room. That inserted some hope of a positive outcome for me. He led us to the third floor and opened the door. It could be best described as "simple," but my mind jumped to words like "desolate" and "old."

Two single beds were pushed together on one side of the room to make a larger bed for a couple, though each had its own blankets. In the corner there was a small refrigerator, which would at least hold a few food items and maybe a bottle of wine. There were narrow, ceiling-high doors that opened to a very small patio. It would be difficult for both of us to sit on the patio together, but it offered fresh air and sunlight. The bathroom was clean but worn, the walls were barren. An uncovered pair of light bulbs hung from the ceiling with a pull string.

It was not a four-star hotel and probably not a full-fledged three-star, but we were in Greece and this was a temporary stop. At the 75 euro-per-night price it was a bargain and we needed a place to detail our plan for exploring Santorini. We paid a happy Joseph for two nights.

Sara's expression as we viewed the room reminded me of her face when she saw the first apartment we rented as newlyweds. We were both taking courses at the college and wanted housing near the campus. We rented a convenient, but basic apartment that was only a short walk to our classes. At first glance, it looked like a Motel 6, but after living there a while, it began to feel like home. Like Joseph Stavros' hotel, it was basic, but it served our purpose.

As Joseph left the room and shut the door behind himself, I turned to Sara. "Are you happy with this?"

Her face crinkled into a smile. "Am I happy with the room? Sure! It'll be fine. Am I happy to be off the ship and in Greece with you? I'm ecstatic—I couldn't be happier."

"No one will ever accuse of us of not being adventurous after this."

"We've only just begun!"

She could have made a case for finding a nicer hotel, but Sara never let little things get her down. "Looking for the positives," she called it. After all, why let a cheap hotel ruin a dream stay in Greece? The hotel was good! Life was good!

As for me, it fit the budget.

"I think I need a nap," she said when she'd finished unloading her bag.

"I can think of something else to do in the bed," I hinted.

Sara's laugh turned into a yawn. "Later, I really do need a nap. The last few hours have been nerve-wracking. You go out and find us food and a bottle of wine for later. Go explore."

"Sounds like a plan." I kissed her and headed out the door. "I'll be back in an hour or so. Sleep tight."

I closed the door softly and headed down the steps. They were worn and uneven, but certainly provided a bit of Greek charm. I walked out into a vacant parking lot near the hotel entrance. The far end of the lot was used as a base for taxis. There were drivers mingling in the area and a short line of taxis waiting for future passengers. I watched with interest and wondered how reasonable the fares would be.

Sara normally didn't nap. Her time being a mother had built up her endurance. She'd done it all: worked at the school, took care of our home, drove the kids to practices, assisted with homework, and an array of other things that made her a super Mom.

As I looked beyond the taxis, the bus station was one level below. It was another parking lot, though it was packed with buses and lines of people waiting. It certainly appeared disorganized as I watched a shiny green, very modern looking bus pull into the lot. The driver appeared to be skilled at maneuvering the vehicle, but had some difficulty parking in the small space reserved for it between the other buses. His efforts were hampered by the many passengers that followed him, trying to get to the bus door first.

I noticed a small office on the far side of the lot. A uniformed attendant tried to assist the bus driver by herding the people and providing hand directions to the driver. They were successful in their maneuvering, but the whole process seemed cumbersome, if not comical. I noticed each bus had a different destination city listed on the front panel. This would be a great way to get around the island and I was sure it would be less expensive than a taxi. However, we would have to do some homework to deal with the craziness of the bus terminal.

Everyone seemed to be in a hurry. After so many years of splitting duties between being a school principal, father, and husband, it felt strange to watch the commotion of the bus station. After only a few weeks away from work, it was like retirement had removed me from that frantic pace of life. I wanted to avoid the chaos and the crowds. It was good to be away from the routines and daily concerns.

I watched the confusion in the bus lot as I walked past on the upper street. I was moving away from the city center where the concentration of tourist shops was very high. I decided to wander in the opposite direction, hoping to find a food market to buy a few items for my evening with Sara. We didn't care much for fancy dinners with high price tags. We preferred quiet time together enjoying simple meals. A cheese plate, a loaf of bread, and a bottle of wine would be perfect for the two of us tonight.

In fact, I had fond memories of buying the same three items on our honeymoon in Hawaii. We'd hiked down to a secluded beach where I surprised Sara with a picnic. We spent hours lying on the white sand, listening to the waves wash ashore, and enjoying the post-wedding time together. We both think back to that day whenever we sit down to enjoy wine, bread, and cheese.

Strolling along the street that appeared to be leading to the edge of town, I spotted a small market. When I went inside, I noticed that most shoppers were carrying their own cloth shopping bags. I assumed that they made frequent trips to the market during the week. They all appeared to know each other and acknowledged each other as they moved about the store, though most of the conversation was in Greek.

I went to look at the cheeses. There were many from which to choose. I scanned the packaging, but couldn't find any familiar brands or words. I decided to select two. The first looked like feta, which I knew both of us liked and certainly was a very popular cheese in Greece. The other, Kasseri, I knew nothing about, but it was one of the few yellow cheeses. I couldn't guarantee that Sara would enjoy the taste, but all these years of marriage to such an adventurous woman, made me confident that she'd at least be willing to try it.

I then moved towards the wine. I wanted to select a local wine. The prices were low—most were around five euros. I selected a white wine from the Santo winery, the label indicated it was a local Santorini vintner. My last selection in the store was a freshly baked loaf of bread. The one euro loaf would be perfect for the two of us.

I was looking forward to a relaxing evening. Sara was right. It had been a stressful day. We'd turned it into a stressful afternoon the second we decided to jump ship.

I headed back to the hotel. As I retraced my steps, the taxi drivers were still mingling. I noticed a couple of taxis drive away with passengers. As I glanced down to the lower level, the bus station was still a madhouse. People scurried from one end to the other, following the buses as if they had a magnetic pull. The walk had enabled me to find some dinner and to survey some of our transportation options for the future.

I'd been gone about forty-five minutes. I approached our room quietly and opened the door very slowly, but the old door squeaked anyway. As I peeked in, Sara was just coming out of the shower. A towel was loosely draped around her.

"I'm up and took a shower to refresh," she said. I grinned when she dropped the towel and gave me a big hug.

"What a great way to start the evening!"

"I generally do that for gentlemen who come calling with wine. What did you get us?"

"The usual...a nice bottle of wine, two cheeses, and some bread."

Sara quickly dressed. "Perfect timing. I'm starving and sunset is about fifteen minutes away."

I poked my head out to look at the little balcony. "I'm not sure we'll see much from here. It looks like the building next door will block our view to the west."

"Where else can we go?" she asked.

"I saw a stairway on my way back to the room that went up toward the roof. Let me go check it out." I wandered down the hall and up a set of stairs. At the top there was a small, roof-top patio. It contained an empty hot tub that was definitely out of service and a stack of older patio chairs. It was a messy area, but I could see the sun on a westerly course. This spot would have a fairly good view of the sunset. I dusted off a couple chairs and hurried down to retrieve Sara.

In less than five minutes, Sara was on the roof unpacking our bread and cheeses, using a towel from our room as the tablecloth. I was already seated on one of the old patio chairs, uncorking the wine. Like an established routine in our relationship, we set up our evening snack and were each holding a glass of wine. "Yamas" followed the familiar clink of glasses.

We watched the sun squeeze between two buildings and slink under power lines. It wasn't the perfect spot, as it would be on the caldera rim, but it was perfect for us.

We watched the red sky change colors with the movement of the sun. The clouds were signaling the end of the day with an orange hue. The skies to the east were dark. The streets in the village were dim. Sara snuggled close to me and marveled at the palette of colors in the sky. This sunset was special. Not only was it a Greek sunset, it was the first sunset on our spontaneous adventure. As the sun disappeared below the horizon, we clinked glasses and followed the toast with a kiss. We were relaxed and we were together.

Sunset was my favorite time of the day. The patio in our home faces west. Most nights, no matter how busy we were or what demands were placed on our time, we would sit outside for at least a few minutes and watch the sun paint the sky and slide behind the tree line. Some nights spurred conversation and relaxation. Other nights it was a kiss and then back to whatever we were doing, but on most nights, a sunset provided a pause for the two of us.

After the sun was gone, Sara broke the silence.

"I think we should stay on this island for a week. That should give us enough time."

"What do you want to see while you're here? That's a long time to be away."

She paused, thinking about her reply to my question. "I want to be able to say I know every inch of this island. It's not that big—so we should take our time and explore it."

I smiled. "I think that's possible, after all, we are retired! I believe Santorini is only about three miles wide and maybe ten miles long. We're right next to the taxi stand and the bus station, so tomorrow we can check out transportation options. I'm not sure if we're going to need to rent a car."

"A car might be nice for a day or two, but I don't mind taking the bus."

"Don't be so quick to volunteer to take the bus until you see the congestion at the bus station."

"It'll all work out," Sara said confidently.

We both seemed to relax and take in the serene moment as the sun's last light faded away. The transition from day to night was happening before our eyes.

"Do you ever wonder why we're not divorced?"

"What? No!" I looked at her. "Is something wrong?"

"No." She looked at the concern on my face and laughed. "No—really no! Breathe, Jay. That came out wrong. I just mean so many of our friends are divorced and the ones who aren't have probably thought about it. What are we doing right that a lot of others aren't?"

I took a sip of wine. "Well, I can't say I question something good. I just figure we have it figured out."

"You have what figured out?" she asked.

"Life, marriage...I don't know. You're going to ruin this romantic moment."

"I'm just curious. People say we're the perfect couple, but what makes us a perfect couple?"

"I don't think any couple is perfect, but we have a lot going for us."

"Then it makes me wonder what we're doing right," said Sara with an insistent tone. "I really would like to explore it a bit."

I sighed. It was an interesting question. I'm not sure why it came up on our first night in Greece, but the thought had certainly entered my mind before. Sara and I have had a great marriage for over three decades and it seemed to get better every year. When so many people I know struggled with their relationships and drifted apart, we seemed to float through life enjoying each day and each other.

I looked at Sara. "I'm game! I wonder if anything will change now that we're retired. With the kids finally on their own, there's more time just for us."

Some couples have difficulties when they retire because they feel like they're under each other's feet the whole time. They lack alone time. Others are bored due to the lack of structure in their daily lives. For us, I didn't see it being much of a challenge.

"We could be like Cooper and Abby and move into two separate condos," Sara said jokingly, referring to our friends back home who were having a difficult time with too much togetherness since they retired.

"I don't think that'll be necessary, but there are definitely things we're doing that make our relationship work."

"Honey, what if we explore our relationship and find out after all these years of marriage we aren't right for each other after all this time?" I asked, chuckling.

"Very funny, I don't think that's going to happen, but we can discuss the positive things in our relationship. Just think about it. What makes it work for us?"

I intentionally changed the topic. "Do we have an agenda tomorrow?"

"Well, we're here another night. Tomorrow we should look online for other lodging options and check out a map of the island to see where we want to visit and what sights we want to see."

"That sounds good to me. When I get up in the morning, I'll check out the bus schedule to see if I can make sense of the madness around the bus station."

"We have no set schedule, just an opportunity to explore, Sara reminded me. "It's the opportunity of a lifetime," she said, smiling.

I recognized that smile. She had similar smiles when we got engaged and on the days our kids were born. It flashed on graduations, anniversaries—even at her retirement party. It was a smile that exhibited her true happiness. Each time I see it, I experience the same joyful feeling.

You could tell Sara was settling into her dream. I, too, was eager to experience the island. It was such a picturesque place. I knew from the list of many excursions in our cruise cabin that there was a lot to see and now we had all the time we needed to experience it. We'd be here for a week's stay, rather than a five-hour stop.

We enjoyed our cheeses and bread. The wine was nearly gone. I marveled at the fact that we were on a rooftop in Greece. As darkness surrounded us, it didn't even matter that we were sitting on dirty old patio chairs next to a broken down hot tub. The only sight that mattered was the night sky filled with stars and the moon reflecting on the sea. We seemed relaxed and at peace with our decision to leave the ship.

Sara glanced at me. "This is perfect," she whispered.

I leaned over and put my arm around her. I turned and kissed her squarely on the lips. "Yes, this *is* perfect."

Chapter 5
A Simple Plan

*Life places many demands on our time.
Though this time is limited, we must learn to
set time aside for our relationship. Love will
grow if it is given the time to nurture.*

Sunlight peeked through the crack in the curtains to wake me. The separate bedding allowed me to slide out of bed without disturbing Sara. As I moved through the room, my eyes adjusted to the dim light. I pulled on shorts and a t-shirt while she slept. She'd pulled the sheets up around her shoulders and she lay curled on her side. Her body was beautifully outlined in the light, white linen. I smiled and let her sleep.

The windows in the lobby were open. I squinted through the morning sun and spotted a large coffee pot in the office area. No one was around, but some styrofoam cups were there for the taking. I filled a cup with black coffee and wandered across the parking lot.

As I shuffled along, my mind wandered to the rooftop of the hotel. Sara had expressed that it was a perfect night and I'd had the same feeling. I snickered to myself as I thought about leaving the comforts of the cruise ship for an evening amongst old furniture on a rooftop with a few morsels of food and wine. Most people would think we were crazy, but this simple setting seemed to be one that we thoroughly enjoyed.

It was a beautiful, peaceful morning. The sun was climbing in the sky with no clouds in sight. Across the street, I noticed the shop owners preparing for the day. They rolled up the corrugated metal coverings that secured their shops at night and started setting up displays of clothing, food, and souvenirs. Their actions had purpose, but it all felt relaxed. It seemed so different from the stores and restaurants back home where every movement seemed rushed.

This place understood the idea of a simple life. Merchants always appeared to take great pride in their businesses and dedicated many hours to them. They were up early in the morning, preparing for the day and worked late into the evening until the tourists decided to go to bed; however, they never appeared too rushed and always greeted you with a smile. Their daily life was not easy, but they never seemed to complicate it. Even when they drank coffee, they sipped it slowly, partook in conversation, and enjoyed the people around them.

I wandered across the parking lot. A couple of taxi drivers were standing near their vehicles. They looked unoccupied and seemed interested in my intentions. I walked over to them.

They nodded and greeted me, "Kalimera" (Good morning) in Greek.

"Kalimera," I said. "How much for a taxi to the other side of the island? How many euros?"

One driver quickly pointed to a sign. It was a rate chart for all taxi routes. Specific charges were listed for specific destinations. It appeared all taxis operated under a unified fare rate. I nodded in appreciation. I continued to study the chart. It appeared a ride to the opposite side of the island was about 15 euros.

"*Efharisto,*" I said to thank them and then headed down toward the bus station.

There were very few people in the lot. It was definitely not the madhouse I'd witnessed yesterday; however, it was still early. I briskly headed down the stairs in the direction of the small bus office. The uniformed attendant was sitting in a chair next to the office.

"Kalimera," I said, "How many euros to get to the other side of the island?"

He pointed to the schedule on the side of the office building without speaking. I was immediately struck by the cheap fares listed on the board. A trip to various locations across the island was only about two euros.

I smiled and nodded approvingly to the attendant, not sure of the amount of English he spoke. "Buy ticket here?" I inquired.

He forced a smile, as if he got this simple type of questioning a hundred times a day. In very good English, he responded, "You will buy the ticket on the bus."

I nodded, a little embarrassed. "Great. Thank you very much for your help. Have a good day." I waved goodbye and started back to the hotel.

The bus was the cheapest way to travel. All the buses in the parking lot were very new looking and clean. The seats appeared roomy and comfortable. I scanned the front of the buses. They had their destination listed on the front above the windshield. The locations listed on the buses this morning included Oia, Kamari, and Akrotiri. The names were familiar from the guidebooks and the excursion guides on the ship. I was sure Sara would have no problem with the bus, although I was still concerned about navigating the crowds later in the day.

As I wandered back to the hotel, my thoughts jumped between plans for the day and the details I needed to address for extending our stay. One of my priorities in the next day or two was to reschedule our return flights. I was concerned that on short notice there might be limited seating available or extra fees or limited refund options. I also thought that I should get in touch with Tommy and let him know that we wouldn't be returning for at least another week. His assistance with the plants and the house would be essential, though I was comfortable that things would be taken care of since he was staying at our house.

Only a few tourists meandered through the streets at this hour. The shop owners shouted greetings to other Greeks across the parking lot and passing on the street. They seemed to nod to any others who passed by. I could feel the community gearing up for another busy day catering to the large crowds of tourists.

As I approached the hotel, I looked at my watch. It was 8:15 am. I'd only been gone about thirty minutes. I decided to grab another cup of coffee, sit on steps, and enjoy the morning. I also wanted to make sure Sara had her needed sleep time. Yesterday seemed to leave her exhausted.

My view consisted of the nearly empty parking lot and a nearby street lined with shops. I was surrounded by some potted plants along the hotel steps and faded white walls. I relaxed on the worn, rounded steps enjoying my second cup of coffee.

Joseph, the hotel owner, touched my shoulder from behind and greeted me, "Kalimera."

"Oh hey, kalimera," I replied, jumping a little at his sudden presence.

He smiled. "You plan on staying more?"

"One more night," I said.

"Only one more night, but there is so much to see on Santorini. You need more time!"

I laughed a little. "We want to see the whole island."

"Okay, so where will you go?" he asked.

I shrugged my shoulders, "Where would you suggest we go?"

He thought for a moment. "Do you like the beach?"

"Yes." Sara and I always thoroughly enjoyed a trip to the beach and I always enjoyed seeing Sara in a bikini.

"Then you must go to Kamari Beach—beautiful black sand beach with many restaurants nearby. Great Greek food and plenty of local wine. You should stay here longer, but if you must go, you should go to Kamari."

"We will, thanks."

Joseph headed into his office and I leisurely finished my coffee, watching the shops prepare for the waves of tourists. It was a sunny morning and I had certainly enjoyed my quiet time.

On my way back up to our room, I grabbed my third cup of coffee and an extra cup for Sara. I approached the room slowly and opened the door quietly, trying not to spill my coffee or wake Sara. Once I poked my head inside, I saw that the curtains had been pulled open and sunlight was streaming into the room.

Sara was awake. She was still in bed, but sitting propped up on a mound of pillows and reading on her iPad. She was partially bare from the hips up. I thought for a moment that she looked like a Greek goddess with the sun shining on her naked body with the sheets pooled around her waist and over one shoulder like a toga. She took off her reading glasses and held out her hand for her cup of coffee. "Good morning. Thank you for bringing me coffee."

"Good morning, my beautiful, rested wife," I replied, swinging the door shut behind me. "It's a beautiful day to explore Santorini. Lots of vivid blue sky."

"That's good...and a cup of coffee for starters. Thank you." She patted the bed next to her and I sat down.

"What are you finding on that iPad?" I asked.

"Lots of stuff."

"Anything you want to see?"

"We have another day at this hotel and I think we can wander around Fira for the day. It seems like an interesting city. I found a place on the other side of the island called "Kamari Beach." It looks beautiful. There's a beach and the restaurants line a walkway. The reviews say it has great food options and it's cheaper than in Fira."

"It has black sand too," I interjected.

"How did you know that?" she asked, looking up from her iPad.

"I was talking to Joseph and he said that if we weren't going to stay here, we should go to Kamari."

Sara turned her iPad towards me and said, "Look at these beautiful pictures on TripAdvisor."

I was impressed. The beach was long with hundreds of thatched umbrellas. There appeared to be no shortage of open air restaurants along the beach. If it was cheaper on the other side of the island, I wouldn't argue with that.

"I vote we head to Kamari tomorrow."

Sara set her coffee aside and rolled out of bed.

I couldn't resist playfully slapping her butt. "Hurry up and get ready—Greece is waiting."

She let out a playful squeal and hopped out of my reach. "I'll be ready in eight minutes. Let's find somewhere to eat. I'm starved."

Within fifteen minutes we were heading out of the hotel and across the parking lot toward the main shopping area of Fira. We found ourselves glancing into shop doorways and nodding at the shop owners who greeted us. Their friendliness was coupled with an invitation to browse their goods. There was a wide array of merchandise in the many narrow shops. The jewelry seemed to catch Sara's eyes, especially the gold pieces. I glanced over the Greek cotton dress shirts, but found more amusement in the slogans on the abundant piles of T-shirts. Art highlighted with bright colors was everywhere. The olive oil, spices, wooden bowls, and other local products were categorized in our minds as probable future purchases before we left the island.

The walkways were not marked with names, but we knew the general direction to get to the caldera. We agreed that we wanted to have breakfast somewhere with a panoramic view of the Aegean Sea. Once we made our way through the winding, narrow walkways between the shops, we came to an open area with an incredible view.

The scenery over the caldera appeared in front of us. The morning sun changed the view of the volcanic rock, varying the colors and the shadows. The early rays spotlighted different sections of the rugged caldera walls. The views to the west were featured as the sun rose higher in the east. The waters, which yesterday were dark blue, appeared to be garnished with a greenish tint this morning; yet they seemed to shimmer into a sparkling blue as they met the pale powder blue of the distant sky.

It created a calming effect that could stop anyone in their tracks. The view takes voices away and forces onlookers to pause and stare. Though we had sat on the caldera rim yesterday and watched over the same view, we were both overcome with its beauty. We both realized that nature's pallette had provided an altered picture of this natural wonder.

The pause ended when Sara pointed out that another cruise ship was in port. We noticed the tender boats jockeying for position as they prepared to bring passengers to the Old Port. "It's so good to be here and not waiting to be shuttled to the port."

"I know," I said, giving her a quick hug before moving down the walkway. The boat definitely was a reminder that only yesterday we'd left the cruise, yet from our perspective high above the port, we felt good about our decision. Our eyes followed the ship as it moved into position in the center of the harbor.

Sara returned us to our purpose with one word: "Breakfast."

We both glanced up one side of the path along the caldera and then the other. There were plenty of restaurants to choose from. The one above us was fitted with large fancy tan-colored umbrellas and matching chairs. It was also packed with people. One down to our left was very cute with dark blue chairs and blue-trimmed tables. It too had several customers.

The one right below where we were standing was a small restaurant patio with six tables. Despite not having umbrellas, it looked like a pleasant setting and it had an uninterrupted view of the cliffs. There was only one other couple and they seemed to be enjoying the breakfast. We decided to avoid the crowds and go with the simple option.

We walked into the patio area and a young woman smiled at us. "*Guten tag.*"

"Good morning," I said. "Table for two?"

"Oh, English," she responded, effortlessly switching languages. "Excuse me, your blond hair and long height made me think you were German. Come, follow me. I'll get you a table. Where in USA are you from?"

"We're originally from the upper Midwest, Wisconsin," Sara told her.

"Oh! I have cousins in Chicago. It gets cold there. Please, sit here, this table has a very nice view. Here is a menu. Take your time." She smiled and left us.

"This is perfect," Sara said. She heaved a big sigh and sank into her chair.

"Perfect. Haven't I heard you say that before?"

Her eyes closed. "Hmm....probably, but I'm enjoying this."

"You are...and so am I. Retirement feels pretty good right now."

That thought brought a content pause to our conversation. Life really did seem perfect.

After a few moments, I playfully interjected, "I think the answer to your question is 'simple.'"

"The answer to what question?" Sara asked.

"The question about what makes our relationship work. Why we aren't divorced."

"Oh, that question," she said, probably remembering that I'd steered her away from that conversation last night. "Okay, if it's so simple, then what is it?"

"It's 'simple'" I repeated.

She frowned. "Simple what?"

I laughed. "Sara, I'm saying we find happiness in simple things."

She sighed. "Well, you could have said that."

"I thought about it. I started noticing how every time the universe seems perfect, we're doing something simple, like sitting on the caldera wall, sitting on old furniture on a rooftop, and even here, we chose the plain restaurant over more elaborate ones."

"Maybe I'm just a cheap date," she laughed.

"Seriously, Sara, I think it's nice that we don't need to do something fancy or spend lots of money to enjoy each other."

She shrugged. "I don't disagree. I just thought that you'd say something like 'compatibility' or 'commitment.' Simplicity just caught me off guard. It's true, though."

I settled back into my chair and faced the harbor. "Compatibility and commitment sound like textbook terms you'd hear on Dr. Phil. They're too vague."

We'd moved so quickly into our discussion that we'd forgotten about breakfast. The waitress returned and stood by our table. We hadn't even opened the menus.

"Have you decided?" she inquired.

We glanced at each other. Sara skimmed the menu quickly and ordered a coffee Americana and Greek yogurt.

Eager to get back to our conversation, I duplicated the order and the waitress left to submit our requests to the kitchen.

"Besides," I said, "It doesn't do any good to figure out if we're compatible at this stage. We've been together for thirty-five years."

She nodded. "I think that covers commitment too. Thirty-five years says something."

"Exactly. Save commitment and compatibility for the talk shows and dating sites. You asked what works for us; this is specific."

"Last night was simple. We rented a 75 euro hotel room that had no frills. I spent fifteen euros on a bottle of wine, cheese, and bread, and then we went up to a messy rooftop with a beautiful view of the sunset that included a power line running right through the middle."

Sara nodded. "And it was perfect!"

"What made it perfect?"

"First, Jay, you have to look at it positively. You're focusing on the cheap, negative side of this. It's not the money. I think you've recognized something about simplicity. Look at the overall situation with a positive attitude. We were at a hotel on Santorini, sitting under the stars with wine and no one else around. Did we really need a fifty euro bottle of wine to enjoy it?"

"Well, when you put it that way, it does sound better."

At that point our breakfast arrived. We smiled and thanked the waitress. Sara stirred her coffee with a disapproving look. As in most Greek restaurants, the coffee was freeze-dried Nescafe. It was not the brewed coffee we had earlier this morning or at home.

Sara leaned in close to me. "Instant coffee might be too simple," she whispered.

I grinned. Whatever the coffee was lacking, the yogurt made up for it. It was rich and creamy with honey drizzled over the top and various nuts sprinkled around the edges. Greece is known for its yogurt and this certainly lived up to its reputation.

After taking her first bite of yogurt and uttering a long "Yummmmm," Sara thoughtfully added, "Being with you made last night perfect. We seem to have a knack for being able to enjoy the simple pleasures of life."

I watched her as her mind seemed to sort through the thoughts in her head. She was beautiful, sitting in the chair with Santorini scenery in the background. I smiled and couldn't help snapping a picture. We ate in silence for a moment, watching the sea.

"The tender boats are starting to take passengers from the ship," I pointed towards them as I scraped the last bit of delicious yogurt from my bowl. Sara glanced over and nodded. She was happy to be off the ship.

I thought about our son, Tommy, and his wife. As well as I knew them, I really didn't have any insight into their life as a couple. Did they take time to enjoy simple things? They did venture out to some nice restaurants and a few nightclubs, but I'm not sure if the rooftop setting would be right for them; yet, I was amused at how well it worked for us.

"We enjoy simple things. I'm not sure everyone can. Some people want to impress—need to impress each other. Maybe too many people just don't take the time to enjoy simple moments, the simple things that life has to offer."

"Well, the Greek restaurants could take the time to put a little more effort into their coffee," Sara said. "I miss my brewed coffee."

I laughed and looked back at the caldera. "Oh no, look," I groaned.

"What? Where?"

"Look in the harbor."

A second cruise ship moved slowly towards the port. The tender boats were already bringing 3,000 passengers off the first ship to Fira, but another ship meant that there would be 6,000 passengers milling around the streets.

Sara sighed. "Well, it's a popular port, I guess."

That many people would definitely change the atmosphere of the village. "It'll take the passengers a while to get off the ship. There's still time to have the island to ourselves."

Sara thought for a moment. "We can wander around the shops for a while after breakfast and take the caldera walkway to Fira Stefani, the next village around lunchtime. Not too many cruise people will wander down that far. They'll want to stay near the shops in Fira."

"A lot of them will be on an excursion following their guide around the village or boarding buses to other parts of the island," I added.

Sara pushed her empty yogurt bowl to the center of the table and moved her half-empty cup of coffee off to the side. She leaned back in her chair, still admiring the view. "So is this one of our simple moments?"

"Ah, Grasshopper, now that you recognize the simple moment, you will be able to enjoy," I said, giving it my best David Carradine impression.

"Ha, ha," she said, making a face. "I think we do this every day at home."

I raised my eyebrows. "Not with this view."

"No, but think about having coffee in the mornings and chatting a little before the day starts. That's simple. Even back when we were rushed getting ready for work and kids packed for school, we had ten minutes together and chatted before waking the kids. I really enjoyed that."

"I did too. It wasn't much time, but it hit the pause button during the busiest time of our lives. It made us slow down when everything seemed to be rushing by so quickly. I think it was good. It gave us a little time to ourselves, certainly better than running our separate ways to Starbuck's."

"Tommy and Anna seem to do that," Sara added.

I choked on my coffee a little. "Yep, they do get busy," I quickly inserted, hoping to detour the conversation.

She continued on as though I hadn't spoken. "They don't seem to hit the pause button and take the time to have a simple cup of coffee together."

"Cut them a break, dear. They have busy lives," I said, punctuating my sentence to indicate the discussion should end.

"Well, they need to take a step back and maybe break their morning routine."

"I know it's their life, but a little time for themselves certainly wouldn't hurt."

"I guess we have a knack for creating some sharing time. I think back. Remember when it was our habit to pause for a hug when passing each other in the hallway? That takes like three seconds, but it made such a difference. Some days it kept me going," Sara added.

"Well, I'm not sure what you were looking for in exploring our relationship, but I do think we have a knack for enjoying the simple moments in life with each other."

"I know we have and I just want to dig a little deeper to understand our relationship. I have to admit this is not what I initially expected to focus on, but thanks," replied Sara.

"Now, before we leave this restaurant, I may have jokingly made the grasshopper comment, but can we define 'simple'? I asked.

"Ah ha! So simple may not be so simple?"

"Okay, I deserve that, but we should define it?" I reiterated.

Sara thought about it, and then said, "It probably could be many things, but to me it's finding opportunities to be together, to relax and enjoy the moment. No need to complicate with fancy dates or dinners. You just need to enjoy what's around you and make the most of what you have."

"I agree. We embrace what we have and seem to enjoy it together."

Sara smiled. "Everyone should be so lucky to embrace what they have."

The waitress removed the empty bowls and cups, and then left the bill for us. We both gazed off over the caldera rim, dedicating time to enjoy the view for few more minutes before leaving. As troubling as it was to see a second ship arriving in the port, it looked majestic. The white paint brilliantly reflected in the sun. It glided effortlessly far below us, as if moving closer to its mate.

Soon the tender boats were scurrying into position, the bright morning sun highlighting their movements. The water that streamed from behind them looked like a brush stroke of white paint across the surface of the sea. The bright colors filled our visual senses, but their movements from this distant perch were silent.

The waitress returned with our change. I stood up and got ready to leave. "We have one more night with Joseph, then is the plan to head down to Kamari?"

Sara grimaced. "I think we should go to Plan B."

"And that would be?"

"We should get our things from Joseph's hotel and leave for Kamari today."

"Today? Forget the second night at Joseph's hotel?"

Sara slipped her arm through mine as we walked.

"It's going to get crowded. Let's ditch the tourists and go to Kamari to settle in."

"You've got a knack for jumping ship! You better not make this a habit or we're going to run out of funds."

She started to sputter an indignant explanation.

"It's fine—I'm with you. It's only 75 euros and we'll leave the crowds. Plan B it is." We walked arm in arm back to the hotel.

As we walked along the caldera pathway, I couldn't help but focus on the two cruise ships far below in the harbor. I knew Sara's plan was a good idea. The 2,000 residents of Fira would soon have another 6,000 guests wandering the narrow streets. It was a good time to pack our bags head to Kamari.

"I'm glad that we can enjoy the simple things. Even when life gets complicated, it seems simpler being with you."

She hugged my arm. "Maybe marriage isn't simple, but simple things can help build a marriage."

Chapter 6
Seeking Support

Every person is a unique individual. Relationships are about two individuals supporting each other to become stronger. Couples who embrace this will grow and evolve together.

"Marriage is not simple, but simple things can help build a marriage." Sara's words lingered in my mind as we stood in the middle of the bus station parking lot. We'd built a successful marriage on a foundation of enjoying simple things in life. Like a fine wine, our marriage had improved with age; however, with our conversations focusing more and more on the success of our marriage, I started to dwell on the fact that I was keeping something from Sara. Secrets weren't simple and they certainly could complicate a relationship. Her words echoed in my head.

We had taken time in the hotel to repack our backpacks and were ready to move on to the town of Kamari. The crowds of people from the cruise ship were gathering and jockeying for position to board the local buses. Their urgency was palpable in the air as they checked their watches again and again to make sure they weren't wasting their precious time away from the ship.

The buses would slowly and cautiously move to one side of the lot, make a "Y" turn and back into a designated parking spot. As the bus moved, the crowd moved. The lot attendant would yell at the crowds to back away and motion to the bus driver at the same time to assist with the parking. When the bus halted in its stall, the crowds formed a line, more like a bunch, outside the door. The door would open and people would shoulder their way to the front like rugby players. As chaotic as it had appeared from the sidewalk above, it was worse standing in the middle of it.

Even within the throng of people, my thoughts hung on the word "simple." We had always said our marriage seemed simple, but in reality I knew all marriages had some difficult times. If fact, my heart sank as I thought about our son and his wife.

It seemed like only yesterday we watched Tommy, our oldest, walk down the aisle with our precious daughter-in-law, Kathy. Their faces glowed as they shared their wedding day with family and friends. Sara was the proud mother of the groom. She was happy to see her son in love.

The next bus pulled into the lot. The sign above the driver's head said, "Kamari." We immediately moved toward the bus, but kept a distance from the gathering crowds. We calculated where the door would align in the parking stall and staked out our position.

I instructed Sara, "Give me your pack and you work your way onto the bus. Save me a seat." She nodded and handed me the handle of her rolling pack before turning sideways to slide her shoulder toward the front of the line. She smiled at me and gave a determined push forward.

Kathy was like another daughter to Sara. The two of them had grown so close over the past three years that Kathy called her "Mom." Our daughter-in-law was a confident woman with a college degree. When she spoke, Kathy projected a sincere, caring attitude. Sara felt that Kathy was a perfect match for her shy, sweet son.

I watched Sara push and climb her way up the steps of the bus. I waited my turn in line knowing that Sara would reserve a seat for me. With a few nudges of the packs and some annoyed looks from those next to me, I boarded the bus and saw Sara waving at me from the sixth row.

"Nice job," I said, sitting down next to her and pushing the bags above the seats.

"No problem. I've got you covered."

Maybe I wanted marriage to be simple for the moment to protect Sara because I was keeping something from her. It was difficult to do and my conscience reminded me that it was. Even though there was not much we could do as parents, I didn't want to derail Sara's dream. I didn't want her to rush off the island to return home, so I decided to keep the information from her a little longer.

We both sat comfortably in the cushioned seats. The mass transportation in Greece appeared to be efficient and inexpensive. The bus ticket taker walked down the aisle selling tickets like a railroad conductor. He greeted each passenger, made appropriate change, and issued a small ticket indicating that each person had paid the 1.60 euros fare. The mood on the bus was relaxed – certainly different than the competitive actions in the boarding area. Sara and I eagerly glanced out the bus window as it pulled away from the station.

As we rounded the corner and headed out of town, I pointed out to Sara, "That's where I bought the wine and cheese last night."

"Cool. It was good stuff."

"Just good? Not perfect?"

Sara slipped her hand into mine. "It was perfect."

I squeezed her hand to let her know I agreed.

But thoughts continued to swirl in my mind. *Why did it seem so easy to please Sara? Why was our marriage successful?* The ritual of wine, bread, and cheese was almost redundant in our relationship, but she always welcomed it and never seemed to want more. It was a simple gesture and to be honest, at times I felt our marriage really was simple – for us anyway, but my thoughts kept coming back around to the kids. *Why had they drifted apart so early in their marriage?*

The bus wound its way down from Fira as it headed in an easterly direction towards Kamari. It was only about five miles from Fira and being at sea level, the change in elevation would happen quickly. We noticed a few wineries and many plots of grapes. The vines appeared to grow in circular clumps rather than on trellises. Most of the homes were small, weathered by the sun and chiseled away by the salty air.

The island did not appear to have any industry other than agriculture and tourism. Judging by the crowds coming off the cruise ships, the tourism industry was thriving. Though I appeared to be looking out the window, I realized I was clearly focused on Sara. She looked content and was enthralled with the glimpse of daily life on Santorini.

"We'll have time to explore when we get off the bus," I said drawing her out of her daze.

"I'm going to love it," she said, still staring out the window.

I pondered whether I should share Tommy's secret with her. It wouldn't be easy for her to hear that our son and his wife had separated, so I suppressed my urge to share. This was her week – one that she'd worked her entire career to enjoy.

Suddenly she turned and focused her steel blue eyes on me. "Thank you."

"For what?"

"For being here for me." She squeezed my hand. "For getting off the ship with me. For making my dream come true. I really need this. You don't know how much I need this."

I smiled. "Of course, I'm here for you. Thanks for pulling me into your dream. I probably needed it too."

"You have always supported me – lots of times, big and small. I'm counting on us always supporting each other."

It was such a sincere and meaningful statement, I wasn't quite sure exactly how to respond. I clutched her hand again and said, "Always, 'til death do us part, right?"

She gave me a quick, close-mouthed smile. "Yep, that's what we promised," she said, and then turned her attention back to the peaceful Greek scenery.

The exchange left me confused. Why did she need to make a statement about always supporting each other? Why did she emphasize that she really needed this escape?

She had turned away from me. I watched her intently. Maybe I was reading too much into the remark. After all, I was the one keeping the secret that our son was having marital problems. He shared the news with me the day before we left for our cruise. His eyes were red and watery, but his message was clear.

"Don't tell Mom," he'd said. "It'll just make her sad and ruin her vacation."

I expected he was right, but it was hard to keep it from her. I wanted her to enjoy this trip of a lifetime, but I knew that she'd have to hear about it from one of us. At times I thought it best that she hear it from me and at other times I thought my son should have the chance to talk to her first.

The rumbling of the bus was muffled by the racing thoughts in my head. I knew there was a possibility that Sara had already spoken to Kathy. They were close, but if she'd told her, she certainly didn't indicate that she knew. *Maybe were both keeping something from each other?* Secrets could definitely complicate a marriage.

We peered out the window as the bus approached Kamari. Sara appeared relaxed and I needed to focus on our arrival at the beach.

The bus rolled past a winery and a local brewery. I added them both to my mental list of places to visit. Kamari didn't seem to be an overly-populated beach destination, but rather a simple village with traditional Greek buildings. As we glanced across the open fields and over the rooftops, we saw a couple of blue archways from the church steeples that rose above the skyline. We also caught a glimpse of the Aegean Sea. There were a few storefronts on the edge of the village, but we could see there were many more ahead.

The bus driver announced, "Kamari Beach!"

"Let's take this side street down toward the beach," Sara suggested.

I agreed and we headed downhill toward the water. The street was narrow and could barely fit two cars as they passed each other. A few small motorcycles and scooters slowly weaved by us as we moved in the direction of the water. Their revving motors clashed with the peacefulness of the traditional village. The side street was lined with a mix of restaurants, small markets, and cluttered tourist shops. Workers at many of the shops were busy sweeping and greeting travelers as they passed.

As we reached the road that ran parallel to the long, black sand beach, we stopped. Initially, my eyes focused on the hundreds of thatched umbrellas meticulously lined up, row after row, across the beach. They appeared to stretch along the sea for about a mile down the coast. The beach itself was at least 100 yards wide from the water's edge to where we were standing. The black sand formed a bold outline at the water's edge. There was a huge mountain, a solid rock that jetted hundreds of feet into the air, straight up at one end of the beach, as if it was standing guard.

Sara took a deep breath. "This is what I've been dreaming about," she exclaimed. "Isn't it beautiful?"

I took a deep breath of salt air before responding, "Majestic!"

The beautiful sea seemed to drown out all of my thoughts, leaving me only with the sights and sounds and smells around me. I stood there for a moment, staring, until Sara gently tugged at my arm and refocused my attention on her.

I smiled and we both took a few steps forward. We were on the far north end of the beach and as we started moving south, in front of us we could see that the narrow road ran parallel to the beach. On the left, the road was lined with restaurants, hotels, and shops. On the right side, the restaurants provided colorful cabanas that enabled guests to enjoy beachside dining. The outside seating looked so relaxing as guests casually dined while enjoying beautiful views over the dark colored sand. The aroma of the food drifted through the air. Waiters carried trays across the road from the restaurants to the cabanas. Plates of local fish, grilled squid, and colorful salads were whisked in front of us to the waiting patrons.

The restaurants all appeared to be very well kept and clean, each with a fresh coat of paint. Owners and staff dressed in dark pants and white shirts seemed to be continuously cleaning. The specials advertised on their chalkboards were very reasonably priced and most included an appetizer, entree, and wine.

Our heads swiveled from one side to the other as we scoped out the restaurants, the plates of appealing food, the beach, and the shimmering waters of the sea, shuffling our feet along the pavement, as if we had no real destination.

"Should we walk along the road and go farther down the beach?" I asked, knowing that there was not far to go in the other direction.

"I'd love to," said Sara. "It looks like there are small hotels all along this area too. It would be great to have a beachfront room."

"It would be nice. We can stop and check out prices if we see something we like."

We resumed our leisurely stroll down the road, which appeared closed to most traffic. Each cabana we passed was unique and decorated to match the motif of the restaurant on the other side of the walkway. The restaurant owners stood in the entranceways, pointing at their menu, and inviting us to stop for lunch or a drink. We smiled and thanked them, often saying that we were staying for a while and would stop by later.

We pointed at colorful decorations around the cabanas and the numerous eye-catching entrees being served to customers. One cabana was bright orange and all the canvas chairs and umbrellas matched; another was decorated in lime green, complete with complementing planters and benches. We also passed by a few small, well-kept hotels, all of which had balconies and windows overlooking the black-sand beach.

After making it about a third of the way down the walkway, I asked Sara, "Do you want to check with any of these hotels on their prices?"

She paused and grinned. "I think our first stop should be for a glass of wine in one of these inviting cabanas."

Laughing, I responded, "I was wondering how long it would take you to decide to stop for wine."

"Well, it will give us a chance to talk about a hotel choice and we can enjoy the view for a while."

I had no problem with that. The view across the beach was a vista of beautiful nature, beautiful cabanas, and beautiful people sunning in the lounges.

Sara selected a cabana called "The Spring." Its bright white exterior and interior was highlighted with rust-colored accents and potted geraniums. There were approximately twelve tables of various configurations in the cabana, each with a matching tablecloth, a candle, and a bottle of olive oil. We sat at a table along the rail that fronted the beach.

Immediately we were greeted by the waiter, "*Kalispera*" ("Good afternoon).

"*Kalispera,*" we replied and thanked him for the beautiful table. He offered menus and we inquired about the wine. The waiter informed us that the local white wine was six euros for a half liter pitcher.

"Excellent, that's what we'll have," I responded. They apparently didn't mark up the wine 400% like they do back home.

As the waiter left to retrieve our wine, we paused and took in the view. I could see the sheer rock walls of the mountain over Sara's shoulder. It was incredible. I scanned the beautiful black sand beach. People were relaxing, many on lounge chairs beneath thatched umbrellas, others strolling along the water's edge. The sun sparkled and skipped across the water. The waves made a gentle, hypnotic rolling sound as they pushed tiny pebbles and sand up and down. I could feel my tension and preoccupations drifting away.

The waiter returned with two glasses and a small pitcher of wine. He filled our glasses and set a small platter of olives and bread on the table.

"Complimentary," he said. "Welcome to Kamari."

We were pleasantly surprised and I thanked him in Greek, "*Efharisto.*"

As he left, Sara remarked, "That was very nice of him."

"Greek hospitality. I love this place!" I leaned back and got comfortable in my chair. "This is wonderful, Sara."

She smiled. "I know! It has everything we could possibly want. Look at that beach, all these quaint restaurants and the unique little shops. I love it too. We definitely need to stay here."

I nodded. "What about a hotel? How are we going to pick one?"

"I say we walk down the entire length of the beach when we're done with our wine and when we get to the end, we'll narrow down our selections. Then we can go back to inquire about price and availability."

"Sounds like a plan." I held up my glass and Sara clinked it with her own. I took a sip and then said, "Glad we have that taken care of."

Sara returned to sipping her wine and gazing out at the sea. She looked upward and as if she was talking to the sky, she said, "You know, we have given each other support throughout our relationship. Life can be tough, but it was always easier having each other."

"I'm not sure our life would qualify as tough, Love, but life has been better together."

"We have had lots of things happen in our life. Just think about the deaths in our family, issues with the kids, jobs, schedules, and on and on."

"You mean life!" I quipped.

"Life is, without a doubt, easier with each other's support," she said seriously.

"You're right. Your support certainly has made a difference for me," I said, knowing that her support was not only important to me during those difficult times, but for my career. I never would have been able to advance so far without Sara helping me through it all.

There was a minute of silence. I wondered if she was thinking about Tommy and Kathy. Did she know?

She and Kathy were very close. I wondered if all this talk of "being there" and "showing support" was really about their marriage instead of ours.

I felt a bit of the tension within me and tried to brush it off with a little humor. "You know I appreciate your support of my golfing habit too."

A still somber Sara rolled her eyes. "You dork."

I laughed and got a smile out of Sara. "Seriously though, some of the guys have to get permission from their wives to golf every week and then get nagged and whined at for going. You just tell me to enjoy. It's nice."

"And how many times have you been to the art gallery for an opening with me, gone to a museum, or waited for me to finish a painting class?"

I smiled thoughtfully. "Bottom line is that we are always there to support each other."

Sara beamed. She seemed to enjoy the philosophical discussion on our relationship. We are a couple who has always been there for each other.

We both seemed satisfied with the short discussion as we sipped our wine with the sea breeze blowing in our faces. I saw Sara lean back with eyes shut. I wondered what she was thinking. She breathed deeply and exhaled slowly. I was certain that she knew I would support her, whether it was helping our son or abandoning a cruise ship or anything else life threw at us.

Sara's hair moved rhythmically in the breeze. The rest of her body remained motionless in the shade of the cabana. When she opened her eyes, she again looked up at the sky. "You think we'll always be that perfect couple?"

"Of course." I touched her hand. "Is something wrong?"

She closed her eyes again. "Nope, I just like that thought."

To me, there was no question about our relationship and the support we provided each other. We had a long history to back it up. Now the questioning spurred me to wonder, *Is keeping Tommy's secret the only issue in need of sharing or is there something else? Why would she need affirmation and reassurance of my support?* The thought was there, though I didn't want to blow it out of proportion.

As usual, I set my empty glass on the table first. "Ready?"

"Give me a second to enjoy," she responded still looking totally relaxed. Her facial expression was peaceful with a slight smile. Her eyes were barely open and her body relaxed. She almost appeared to doze off, though I expected rather than dreaming in her sleep, she was just enjoying living her dream.

The waiter walked by and inquired if we would like more wine. I smiled with a quick hand signal indicating no more was needed. He nodded and left us the bill. I thanked him in Greek and glanced at Sara. She appeared ready to move on.

"Shall we?" I asked pulling back her chair and assisting her to her feet.

"Yes. This is a great place."

I could see she was taking in everything around her. The pleasure showed on her face and helped ease my concerns.

~~~

We headed back to the narrow road along the beach. Several other restaurant owners offered us seating, but we smiled at each and indicated that we had just stopped.

Our focus was now on the many small, family-owned hotels nestled in among the restaurants and shops on the roadway. Even though they were right across from the beach, many had pools. We paused and looked at a well-appointed hotel. The Greek architecture was highlighted with rust-colored shutters and bright blue doors. The tables on the patio and poolside were colorful and stylish. An inviting courtyard bar served drinks. The chaise lounge chairs were filled with tourists wearing skimpy swimwear, many holding chilled cocktails. Some people sat relaxing on their balconies above.

I wondered if they had a vacancy and looked at Sara. "Should I ask about the price?"

"Stick to the plan," said Sara with some enjoyment, since I was the one who always wanted a plan.

"Okay, just asking."

Sara squeezed my hand. "It's nice, just a little too close to the main area for me. All these people always walking by, I'm not sure if I want to be gawked at by all the strolling tourists."

With that response, I knew we would stroll and continue to the end of the road along the beach. Her plan was to carefully examine each hotel, but reserve judgment until we got to the end.

Our mission continued at a leisurely pace. We often commented on features of a hotel—the size of the pool, the comfort of the cushioned beach chairs, the color of the decor, and the vibes of the courtyard. A few stood out as possibilities and some were taken off our list. Though our remarks and the process were informal, I had a sense that Sara was looking for something specific.

However, to my surprise, her thoughts were not apparently as focused on the hotels as I had imagined. As we passed an older couple who were traveling at a slower, more methodical pace than we were, lovingly clinging to each other's hand, Sara sighed and nudged me with her elbow.

"What?"

"Do you think we'll be like them as we grow older?"

"Why do you ask? Of course we will! Are you worried I won't be at your side post-bikini age?"

"That comment isn't giving me a feeling of support," she quipped.

"Hey, I thought we were only going to talk about the positive factors in our relationship. I'm always going to be there to support you. Don't be so sensitive."

Her demeanor drew my attention, as Sara seemed concerned.

"You know I'll change with age," she said softly.

I put my arms around Sara and hugged her close. "No worries. No matter what happens or no matter how many wrinkles you get, I'll be there for you," I said, trying to secure her thoughts and add some levity.

"Promise? Even in a one piece swimsuit?" she said with a calming smirk, still embracing me.

"Promise. Always. We'll age together, you know. We always have." Her question unsettled me. There seemed to be an urgency mixed in the humor of her continued questioning. What was the issue? I could sense there was something.

She backed away from me, took a reassuring breath, smiled, and the sparkle returned to her eyes.

We continued our walk. I couldn't leave the topic alone. I needed some closure. "You know we've made it this far in our relationship supporting each other. I think it's safe to say our relationship is strong enough to overcome a few wrinkles." She looked at me and said, "Thanks, right now that's important to me."

She redirected the conversation. "But right now, we need to find a hotel." She squeezed my hand again and we moved on. The exchange left me with an unsettled feeling.

We returned to our assessment of the hotels. We had walked for quite some time but hadn't really made much progress regarding our selection. There were many that were appealing, but only a few that we thought had a chance of being in our price range. There were others we had eliminated. We wanted to have a hotel a bit more upscale than Joseph's, but still a small, traditional hotel.

As we neared the end of the walkway, Sara stopped abruptly. She paused and scanned the small hotel in front of us. It was white with dark blue trim and doors. Purple bougainvillea climbed the trellises around the balconies that overlooked the courtyard. There was a small, five stool bar near the pool. A couple of guests chatted with the bartender. A few more people enjoyed the sun in very comfortable looking lounge chairs. It was a postcard for Greece come to life.

"This one looks perfect!" She winked, knowing the word 'perfect' was quickly becoming an inside joke.

"It does!" but then I asked, "Is it too close to the walkway?"

"No, it's down on the end with less traffic. It's adorable!"

We walked into the hotel courtyard and were immediately greeted and welcomed by a young 20-something bartender, as well as by the other guests sitting at the bar. The first impression and the sincere welcome spoke highly of the hotel. The bartender introduced herself as Evie, her beautiful dark features highlighting her Greek ancestry. She explained that her parents owned the hotel, which was named "The Boathouse."

"Come sit at the bar," Evie requested. "I'll tell you a little about the hotel."

We accepted her invitation and she quickly set a glass of white wine in front of us. I reached for my wallet to pay, but she motioned it away. "It's on the house."

I smiled, thinking *I could really get used to this Greek lifestyle.*

As we were getting settled in, Evie's mother came out of the hotel office. Evie informed her that we were looking for a room. Her mother quickly introduced herself as Diane and warmly welcomed us to the hotel. Her hair was dark, her English was impeccable, and her smile inviting. The other guests at the bar chimed in and told us how wonderful and friendly the hotel was and about the great breakfast they had in the morning. Diane chuckled at their salesmanship and offered to show us a room.

She took us to the far side of the hotel. "You're in luck," she said. "We have a wonderful room on the second floor available."

We entered the room. It was rather large, but somewhat sparse. However, I noticed a king-size bed and glanced at Sara with an approving smile. This was definitely an upgrade from Joseph's hotel.

We looked around, examining other features of the room. On one wall was a colorful painting of a boat and some natural rock decorations that gave the room some character. The floor was beautifully tiled and there was a small refrigerator in the corner. We didn't say much about the room because the owner, who obviously took great pride in her lodging, was with us.

Diane may have sensed some hesitation from our lack of comments because she moved to open the French doors that opened to the balcony. Our eyes immediately focused on the stunning view. It overlooked the pool and out over the beach. The sea glittered beyond the beach. Bougainvillea flowed over the lattice and around the balcony, which was large and extended the entire length of the room, with a table and two chairs. It was at least five times the size of the small balcony at our last hotel.

Sara stepped out onto the balcony. "This is Greece!" she said with certainty.

Diane laughed and affirmed, "It is and this should be your room."

"I love the balcony and the view," Sara said.

Being the realist, I asked, "How many euros a night is this room?"

"120 euros a night."

It certainly was a fair price, if not a bargain. I was about to tell Diane we'd take it but before I could, Sara responded, "Great, we'll take it for a week!"

Diane smiled at me and I nodded. I put my arms around Sara in a supportive hug. "Well, our adventure now has us staying at the Boathouse Hotel for seven nights."

Chapter 7
Blue is the Color of Greece

Spending time together in a relationship is only part of the equation to understanding each other. Couples must consciously set time aside for the purpose of having meaningful communication and to focus solely on each other.

I caught myself staring into the flame of a tea light that was flickering behind navy glass. It lit a small area of the deep blue tablecloth which covered our table in the Almira Restaurant. It was a reflective moment. The blue flickering candle pushed my thoughts to the unending shades of blue that surrounded me in Greece. Dark cobalt blue domes topped the churches along the caldera, standing out like beacons in the sun and disappearing at night. The doors and trim of many of the buildings was the same bold, vibrant blue, commonly referred to as "Greek Blue." Even the railings of this restaurant by the sea were doused in the same blue.

It was a quiet moment. Neither of us spoke. My mind floated away. The azure water of the Aegean Sea was splashing in my mind. Its hues changed with the time of day. The deep turquoise waves that washed gently ashore this afternoon with such a calming effect had given way to the mysterious lure of the darkening waters. The moon sprinkled white light on the churning waves. The continuous rolling motion of the water mesmerized me until an unusually loud crash against the shore seemed to re-focus me. I glanced away from the water to the blue and white Greek flag waving gently in the breeze outside the restaurant, its blue representing the country's water and sky, the white representing its waves and clouds.

Maybe that's why Sara's steel blue eyes caught my attention. They were only three feet away from my face, but they seemed so distant. Her thoughts appeared to be elsewhere, maybe drifting across the darkened blue sea waters as mine were. The restaurant was on the beach near the water's edge. The cabana, softly lit in the open air, provided a romantic setting. Though we sat across from each other, our thoughts seemed to wander with the breeze.

A soft smile came over Sara's face as the waiter walked up behind her and placed a light blue shawl over her shoulders. She welcomed the warmth that the shawl provided and graciously thanked him. This was evidently a customary practice since the sea breeze was often cool in the evening. Sara clutched the shawl around her body and gave an approving smile. Her brilliant blue eyes reflected the light of the moon and the tea light.

The waiter had welcomed us to the restaurant and had suggested starting with a carafe of local white wine. Since one of our goals was to experience the local offerings and wine was on our agenda, we welcomed his suggestion. He then asked the all-important question, "Would you prefer a half liter or a full liter?"

Sara and I exchanged a mischievous glance. I replied, "The full liter, please."

To us, the larger portion of wine meant that we would take extra time to relax and enjoy our time in the restaurant together. Wine was a conversation starter, one of those simple pleasures and apparently a staple of our diet. As the waiter left to retrieve the wine, we were both staring at the blues around us and breathing in the soft sea breeze.

I reached across the table and grasped Sara's hand. She rewarded me with a gentle squeeze of her warm hand and a reassuring smile. "You seem quiet tonight," I said. I meant it as a question.

"In thought," she responded with a slight smile that was almost a grimace. The smile never reached her eyes and like the waves, washed away a moment later.

"Are you okay?" I asked, wondering if she was having second thoughts about leaving the ship.

"I'm fine," she said. "You don't seem too talkative either."

"I was thinking about how I love the island, the many shades of blue. It seems to be the color of Greece."

Sara's eyes drifted back across the sea. "True. It seems like the whole place is accented in blue."

The waiter returned with a full liter of local white wine. "*Assyrtiko*," he announced as he placed the carafe on the table. He then placed a small glass in front of both of us. The traditional glass looked more like a small juice glass. The waiter promptly filled the little glasses with wine and then asked for our dinner requests. Without much delay or discussion, we ordered a Greek salad and the fresh fish—the special listed on the chalkboard outside the restaurant. The waiter nodded and headed across the roadway to the kitchen.

I stared across the table at Sara. "You look beautiful tonight. The shawl matches your eyes."

She smiled in return, but it was easy to see her thoughts were still drifting away.

The waiter soon returned with some finely blended traditional fava dip, freshly baked bread, and a large bottle of olive oil. "To enjoy with your wine," he said, leaving them at our table and exiting with a friendly smile.

We both appreciated the gesture and thanked him as he departed. I waited for Sara to take the first piece of bread. She loved fava, which in Greece is made from finely ground yellow split peas. However, instead of helping herself to the bread right away, she took a sip of her wine.

"You don't want the fava dip? Are you sure you're okay?" I asked, a little humor creeping into my voice.

"I'm fine," she responded, managing a reassuring smile. "Just feeling a little...well, a little blue, I guess."

"What's wrong?"

"Nothing."

"Can I help?"

"No." She sighed and glanced away. "There are just a few things at home I need to get to and I guess you caught me thinking about them." Her voice sounded final, as if she wanted to end the discussion. I was troubled because her dream was to be sitting here enjoying the romance Greece had to offer and yet she seemed so uneasy. I wondered again if she knew about the kids separating.

I squeezed her hand again. "I can help make a few calls or get some friends to take care of whatever it is. Are you worried about your plants? Did you forget to pay some bills?" I paused. "I can help."

Sara leaned forward and picked up a piece of bread and dipped it in the fava. She looked in my direction and the soft waves of her smile touched the edges of her eyes. "It's nothing. Let's just forget about it. You're sweet. I love you."

I put on a serious face and asked, "But do you love the fava?"

Sara took a bite. "Yes, it's delicious." She tried to keep a straight face, but a small laugh escaped.

I patted her hand before taking it away to get some food. "Seriously, Sara, look at this place. It's beautiful. We're by the sea—on Santorini! Whatever's back home is back home. Enjoy our time here, but if I can help, just let me know."

She smiled. "I will set my concerns aside."

"Let's enjoy the wine."

"To all life has to offer!" she said raising her glass.

We touched glasses. "*Yamas.*"

It was a reminder to me that whatever concern we each harbored, it was now time to focus on each other and the adventure we had pursued by leaving the ship. My own thoughts had wandered throughout this trip, thinking about Tommy and Kathy, the details about extending our trip, and now I was trying to get inside Sara's distant thoughts. Her words indicated that there was no need to be concerned, but her body language communicated otherwise.

We set our glasses on the table, the waiter returned with our salad and fish. The salad was a large ceramic bowl filled with cucumbers, tomatoes, and olives, which was topped with a large, thick slice of feta cheese. It was a classic Greek salad. Not only did it look healthy, it was delicious. The fish surprised me. I was expecting a large fillet of fish, maybe sea bass. Instead, there were eight small fish—heads and fins included, all lined up on the platter, garnished with small potatoes. We didn't say anything to the waiter, but adopted an adventurous attitude, each taking one off the platter.

I watched Sara start to organize her plate and systematically start deboning her small fish. I inwardly grinned as I watched this Midwestern woman revert to her roots and prepare this fish for eating. It was as if it was one of her father's fresh-caught lake perch. This routine seemed to set her at ease. Although she remained quiet, she seemed to breathe easier and the far-away look drifted from her eyes. She sat more upright, moving her shawl more off her shoulders and then adjusting her bra strap, apparently for comfort. Her focus and fork moved towards her food.

I pondered what had just happened here. Something was obviously bothering Sara, but she wanted to dismiss it. We have always been good communicators and reached out to each other for support in troubled situations; yet, I was not being the most forthcoming either. There seemed to be issues neither one of us really wanted to address.

The dim candlelight flickered. The slight crackling sound from the translucent blue candle seemed to drown out the distant sea waves and any thought of conversation. I glanced at Sara and her normally vivid blue eyes appeared to be hidden in the shadows of her thoughts.

Sara glanced upward from her plate. She scooped up a mouthful of salad. "I love these fresh tomatoes."

"That's your Midwestern roots," I teased.

She crinkled her nose at me.

I smiled. "The tomatoes are good."

"Everything in the restaurants here is so fresh. I love it!" She took another bite of the salad.

I knew that I should enjoy the moment and this wonderful meal, though I still had thoughts of probing into Sara's concerns.

The meal progressed nicely. We complimented the food and spoke of our travels. We talked about our upcoming time on the island and our hotel. We enjoyed the moment, enjoyed the setting, and enjoyed each other. By the end of the meal, the plate of fish had become a pile of bones and the rest of the bowls were empty. Only the liter of white wine, still half full, had anything to offer. I poured some into the undersized wine glasses and gave a wink. "*Yamas.*"

The waiter cleared the table. Soon we were facing each other across the blue tablecloth with only the flickering blue candle between us. Sara touched the candle with one finger and rotated it. The light danced across her face. She remarked, "I love tea lights. They add atmosphere to anything." She continued to rotate the candle for a few more moments. We both stared at the flickering light and pale blue hue of the candle.

I wondered if this was one of the simple moments in our relationship that drew us together, but sitting in the moonlight watching the waves and the glittering candlelight didn't feel simple. It felt as though there was a small wedge between us separating this moment from reality. There seemed to be something that needed to be discussed, but neither of us wanted to bring it up.

I'd always felt that in our relationship Sara and I always talked openly and honestly with each other. We seemed to know when something needed to be discussed. We had the uncanny ability to take care of things as small issues, rather than waiting for them to grow into something larger. I just needed to decide if this was an issue that needed to be left alone or if this was the time to discuss it.

Sara picked up her wine glass. She leaned back in her chair, snuggling into the warm blue shawl. She seemed relaxed and content. She either felt comfortable about her issues or as she said, had set them aside. "Look at the moon shimmering across the sea."

"It's beautiful," I told her.

Sara took a deep breath and nestled into her chair. She murmured, "It's times like this that we seem to just step away from everything else in life and connect with each other and enjoy the moment."

"It's a good skill we have," I added.

"It makes me think of when the kids were growing up and our schedules were hectic, but we still found time for us. No other concerns, intrusions, or influences from the outside world."

"We made sure the kids were in bed or taken care of," I said jokingly and then added, "but we did know how to set time aside for ourselves and enjoy each other."

"You know what I like about right now and all those other times?" Sara asked.

"What?"

"I like that no matter what's going on in our normal life, in our family's life, or in the entire world, the only thing that matters is that you and I can take the time to just enjoy each other."

I nodded. "Me too." Her words swirled in my head. Something was bothering her, but it seemed clear that she was determined to enjoy the moment.

She was right – we had always been able to set time aside for us. This was a dream-like setting and we needed to focus solely on each other.

I put my elbows on the table and held my wine glass with the fingertips of both hands. I peered over the wine glass and into Sara's eyes. They looked so blue and with the light of the candle reflecting in them, the irises looked like slices of blue glass. I smiled. "This evening has been wonderful. I think we put ourselves into a setting where it was just the two of us. We enjoyed an excellent meal in a very beautiful and peaceful setting. I love spending time with you. I think this together time has always been something we've focused on which strengthens our relationship."

"Time...time together we do well. Do you realize how many times tonight you complimented me on my eyes? Told me I was beautiful? Warmly touched me?"

I laughed. "I hope not too many times."

"Never too many times," said Sara. Her eyes started to glimmer with unspilled tears.

I covered her hand with mine. "You are beautiful."

I filled our glasses with the last of the wine from the carafe. As I set down the empty carafe, I remarked, "You know what I find funny about our discussion?"

"What?" Sara responded.

"We sit here feeling thankful that we've had time to be together and connect, but over the last ten days we have traveled and been with each other all day, every day. Doesn't that seem strange that despite being together almost every minute of each day, we still need time to connect?"

Sara pondered my comment for a moment. She looked somewhat puzzled and then her lips curled into a grin. "I think just being together isn't enough. We needed to set other thoughts aside and just focus on us. If we didn't make time, we'd go about our routine without really understanding or enjoying each other."

"Even on vacation," I added.

Despite our drifting thoughts, we'd found the time to enjoy each other. There may have been things we could have discussed—or should have discussed, but we put them aside. As we continued to talk, my focus was solely on Sara.

Thinking about our earlier discussions I added, "We enjoy simple things in life and that's important in our relationship...anybody's relationship, but being together isn't enough. You need to take time with the purpose of connecting with each other, understanding each other."

"Connecting time," Sara said with a smile and then added, "I very much needed time with you tonight. The setting was so beautiful, the meal so wonderful, but I had things clouding my mind and the time connecting with you helped clear it."

Our conversation continued and I could feel the invisible wedge between us shrink. It was clear that just being together didn't mean that we were really together. We had to make time to connect with each other. We had to talk and listen. We had to devote time for understanding each other.

We were nearing the end of our wine when the waiter set the bill on our table. A small platter accompanied the bill with two very small glasses of *Raki*, a traditional Greek after-dinner drink. We laughed at the sight of the *Raki* and thanked the waiter for a wonderful meal.

He may have sensed that we were going to leave the shots behind, so he interjected, "You must drink the *Raki*. It is good for your digestion." He also added, "It's good for romance and I see that you are a very romantic couple."

We smiled and thanked him for the after dinner treat and his kind words. As we both reached for the small glasses, he smiled and retreated to the kitchen.

"To connecting," I said with exuberance.

Sara clinked my glass. *"Connecting!"*

We sampled our first taste of *Raki*. The taste was bitter and powerful. We tried to conceal our contorted facial expressions from the waiter, wanting to uphold the Greek tradition.

As I set down my glass, I looked over at Sara. Her puckered face was returning to normal and her laughter dispelled her blues. Her spirits from the beginning of the meal had been raised and it wasn't due to the spirits we had just consumed. I reached for her hand and looked directly into her spirited blue eyes. "Serious for a second: This time together has been great, but you seem troubled. Is there anything I can help you with?"

Sara didn't stop giggling and squeezed my fingers. "If I told you that you could help me finish this *Raki*, would that make you feel helpful?"

Her laughter brought a half-smile to my face, "Are you sure?"

"My concerns kind of drifted away tonight. It felt good to set them aside. It's nothing that you can really help with anyway. Some other time. Right now, let's just be here. Connecting time."

I still had concerns, but let them go. "Okay, just let me know if I can help out."

Sara smirked and said in a less serious tone, "You can help by finishing my *Raki*." The evening ended with conversation and laughter, surrounded by the beautiful blues of Greece.

Chapter 8
The Beauty of Silence

Silence is important in a relationship. It can create a tranquil, peaceful setting. It can allow you to enjoy the moment and give you a chance to reflect. Alternatively, silence can be tense. It can create awkward interactions and stop time. Silence can be as forceful as shouting. It can rivet through a person like a barrage of harsh words. Silence is as manipulative as speaking and couples must use silence to communicate positively.

I stood silently behind Sara with my hands resting on her hips. I gently kissed her neck and then rested my chin on her left shoulder. She reached down, clasping her hands on my wrists and then wrapped my arms around her body. I tightened my embrace, cradling her breasts in my hands. Every curve of our bodies seemed to fit together like a puzzle. I could feel the warmth of her body, as well as her love. We stood in silence taking in the moment and the picturesque view. We were standing in the same spot along the caldera where we had decided to leave the ship and stay on the island.

We silently watched a cruise ship making its way into the harbor far below. It seemed to move slowly in the distant water, its size dwarfed by the enormous cliffs. The bright white vessel glided effortlessly far below the caldera rim. It wove between the rugged, black and rust colored volcanic islands that seemed to guard the entrance to the harbor.

"No regrets," I whispered in Sara's ear.

She turned her body towards mine and put her arms around my neck. Her lips were silent, but her eyes seemed to respond with the message I wanted to hear. Pushing up on her toes, pressing her body against mine, her sparkling eyes looked deep into mine. She smiled, "Not one regret."

We embraced tightly, each of us taking an opportunity to glance back at the ship in the harbor below.

We had come to this spot in Fira to begin our six-mile hike along the caldera to Oia. This village on the northwestern tip of the island was known for beautiful vistas and evening sunsets. The hike would allow us to leave the crowds in Fira and enjoy the natural landscape enroute. Sara had done her research and many of the Boathouse guests had confirmed that the hike was a must-do on Santorini.

The beginning of our journey took us through the outer edge of Fira. We walked along the winding cobblestone walkway past shops and restaurants. We even passed the Kafenio Wine Bar without stopping. There were plenty of people in the village and certainly more on the way from the cruise ship. I was glad that we were heading out of Fira. The hiking path undoubtedly would be less crowded as the cruise ship passengers would spend most of their time in Fira or on one of the ship's excursions.

As we made our way farther down the path, we did very little talking. The crowded narrow walkway forced us to walk single file as we wove our way through the gaps in the wandering tourists. We walked quickly and the farther we got from the village center, the easier it was to walk. We wanted to be away from the village buildings where we could enjoy the solitude of the hike, so our pace was brisk.

Sara led the way. She was determined to complete the hike in three hours. I followed, pleased that she had expressed no regrets for her decision to leave the ship and thankful to see that she seemed to set aside her concerns from last night. She moved with a bounce in her step.

The views of the vivid Aegean Sea and the whitewashed buildings were stunning. Sara proceeded along on the narrow cobblestone path. Her shorts were form-fitting and her long legs were toned. She was breathtaking. I would follow her anywhere.

My thoughts churned in the silence. If Sara still harbored the concerns that were apparent last night, she was hiding them well. It seemed as though she felt better as she certainly hadn't had trouble sleeping. I had to wake her up and encourage her to get downstairs and enjoy breakfast before we embarked on our hike.

She made no mention of any issues while we enjoyed coffee and Greek yogurt by the pool this morning. It appeared our time together at dinner really did allow her to enjoy the meal and set any concerns aside. Her focus was on the hike. We discussed the bus schedules and the timeline for our adventure. She was thrilled we were being active tourists and shared our intentions with several other guests.

I watched her with concern and examined my own thoughts. I wanted her to enjoy the trip and our stay on the island without interference from our normal life. Part of the purpose of this trip was to take time away from our regular routine and leave all worries and responsibilities behind. If she knew about the kids and wanted to discuss it, she would have to initiate the conversation. I didn't want to bring it up; yet there still seemed to be another issue that needed to surface.

We headed up a steep, stone stairway between two whitewashed buildings. One appeared to be a hotel and the other a restaurant. Each had a patio that hung over the edge of the caldera with magnificent views of the sea. The restaurant's white umbrellas matched the white tablecloths and chairs. Candles adorned the tabletops, alongside small vases of wildflowers. It was romantic and appealing, but we stayed focused on the hike.

The pace of our walk and the steepness of the stairs sent a burn through my thighs. I glanced up at Sara. Her muscular legs seemed to have no trouble conquering the climb. Her pace slowed very little. I watched her thigh muscles flex and push upward. I did catch a glimpse of her eyes as she glanced back to see if I was keeping pace. I smiled to myself since I was an avid runner and definitely the athlete of the family. Though I was the one toting a backpack containing a few bottles of water and the binoculars today, I made sure that I stayed close behind her.

At some point, I knew we would stop and enjoy our surroundings. I wasn't looking for an opportunity to rest, but I wondered if the pause from hiking would give Sara an opportunity to share. Though I wanted her to know that I cared about her and the kids, I also was curious to know what was on her mind. There were positive and negative outcomes to either bringing up the subject or ignoring the subject. Frankly, it seemed to be bothering me more than Sara. Maybe that's why my gut feeling was to ignore the topic—well at least during the early part of our hike. We continued walking in silence.

There were still buildings on both sides of the walkway; however, I noticed there were fewer souvenir shops. Most of the businesses were now upscale hotels and restaurants. According to the island map I had in my pocket, we were now in the village of Imerovigli. There really wasn't much of a gap between Fira and this village, but the businesses seemed manicured and more upscale. These gave me the impression that they may be out of our price range.

The walkway now wound its way between the buildings in more of a meandering fashion. There was more of a rolling effect to the path that took us up and around businesses and then back down. It was amazing to look back down along the caldera at the maze of pathways that connected the tiers of businesses. The many patios and pools built into the side of the cliffs offered amazing, romantic getaways.

As we hiked up the stairs around the rounded features of a hotel roof, Sara paused to admire the view. She was still silent, but I saw her take a deep relaxed breath. She seemed to be enjoying the scenery. Her eyes glided over the glistening white buildings, following the paths and stairways that led in and out of each establishment. She paused and looked back towards Fira, as if to see what we had accomplished. I paused and glanced back at Fira. We had come quite a ways down the path, although I could still make out the cruise ship sitting in the harbor. It appeared even smaller now that we had moved farther north. The steep sides of the caldera were visible and the view from farther down the coast gave a better perspective of the massive size of the cliffs. The white buildings appeared perched on top of the dark volcanic rock that lined the island wall, which was sparsely dotted with daisies and colorful shrubs.

I reached into my backpack and pulled out a bottle of water. I turned to Sara, held out the bottle and said, "Water?"

Sara took a breath and nodded affirmatively as she reached for the bottle. Her breathing seemed a bit heavier now that we had stopped and she appeared to need the break. She took another deep breath and another swig of water. She turned toward me with her mouth still filled with water and gestured to me to take the bottle. I immediately took a large swallow. The cool water made me realize how thirsty I was.

As I put the cap on the plastic bottle, I felt Sara's arm reach around my neck and pull me towards her. She was one step higher than I was which resulted in my nose being playfully pulled into her cleavage. I made a little snuggling motion and glanced up at her with a smile. Sara's playful smile was accompanied by a giggle. I stepped up onto her step and took my place behind her. I reached my arms around her and put my chin on her left shoulder so that our cheeks touched. There was no need for another word. We held our embrace silently and looked out over the sea. The beauty of Santorini surrounded us and we were taking the time to enjoy it.

I pressed my cheek against Sara's cheek. At the same time I pulled her body towards mine to heighten the embrace. She adjusted my grip and lowered my arms below her breasts. We swayed, ever so slowly, first to the right and then back to the left. I glanced at the front features of my dear wife and then surveyed the rugged features of the cliffs. I enjoyed both views and was in no hurry to move on.

We stood there for at least five minutes. There was no need for words. I had anticipated that at our first stop there would be a dilemma for both of us to address Sara's concerns of the previous night or bring up our son's separation. Yet here we were, embracing and not a word. It wasn't a tense moment. It was a beautiful moment of silence. At that moment I felt more connected to Sara than at any other time today. There was nothing that needed to be addressed.

Finally, I lessened my hold around Sara. She turned and moved so that we were shoulder to shoulder. I tapped her butt as a signal that it was time to move on. Without hesitation, she reached for my hand and started up the walkway. It was wide enough for us to walk side by side, holding hands, for about thirty yards before the path narrowed and into a small, winding stairway. I let go of Sara's hand and she assumed the lead. I fell into position behind her.

I was feeling as if the pause from our hike was a moment that connected us. It was reassuring to me that the long periods of silence this morning were not a result of any issues between us. Sara's embraces certainly brought on a feeling of togetherness; however, I couldn't avoid reflecting on the silence. We'd been hiking for about thirty minutes and I could probably count on one hand the number of sentences exchanged between us. The path moved away from the buildings. The stone walkway was now uphill and lined with a six-foot rock wall on both sides. Our view was limited, but the various wildflowers provided an eye level bouquet of colors.

In our relationship, we enjoyed the quiet times alone, but we also used silence to show our anger. We were not the type to have loud shouting matches or to yell insults at each other. We tended to stop talking if issues were becoming heated. The positive result was that we didn't escalate the issue through frustrated verbal remarks. It usually allowed time for us to calm down, though on occasion the silence festered between us.

The peaceful silence now gave me time to enjoy the scenery. Each turn in the path brought stunning new views. The horizon seemed to change continuously. The sea was the constant factor. The outer islands seemed to slowly shift as we followed the trail. We were circling the cruise ship as we trekked along the semi-circular shape of the caldera rim.

The views continued to change with each step we took towards Oia. I watched people venture out onto their patios that were built into the steep sides of the cliffs. Their sole purpose was to soak in the amazing scenery. There seemed to be nothing more fulfilling than sipping on mid-morning coffee and peering out over the sea.

The silence also enabled me to observe the people passing us on the path. Many were hikers like us. Some were walking in the same direction and others were walking towards Fira as they had begun their journeys in Oia. Their voices represented many languages, as people from all over the world regarded Santorini as one of the most beautiful spots on the planet. I found it fascinating that people from so many different homelands and backgrounds were all here for the same purpose—to enjoy the view. It was fun trying to identify from their conversations where they were from.

Sara also watched the people as they passed and often gave pleasant nods and greetings. She appreciated art and beauty. Her eyes focused on the brightly colored decorations of the patios and storefronts. The colors popped against the white buildings. Sara was in tune to her surroundings. Her body seemed relaxed, but determined to conquer any difficult terrain that we may encounter ahead.

At times, I seemed more focused on Sara than the incredible scenery around me. I knew she was in her element and I was happy that she was enjoying her dream. We were in Greece and it was fitting that my goddess was right in front of me. There was something about the silence that heightened the enjoyment of the hike. It seemed like a perfect opportunity to reflect, while at the same time, enjoy the moment. Today, there seemed to be a euphoric feeling that we were meant to be here.

Ten minutes later, the path emptied into a parking lot. As we continued walking across the lot, we could see a painted rock with an arrow and the word *"Ia"* painted on it. The arrow indicated the continuation of the correct route, but the two-letter spelling of Oia let us share a giggle. During our limited time in Greece, we quickly learned that the spellings of words often vary. This was the third different spelling of Oia today and it's only a three letter word.

Our laughter broke the silence. "Looks like this is the path we need to follow," said Sara.

"High marks for the assistance, but failed on the spelling."

Sara took another sip of water and grinned. "I think anyone could get an "A" on a Greek spelling test—every spelling seems to be acceptable."

As we stood by the rock and peered back towards Fira, we could no longer see the cruise ship in the port. It felt satisfying to leave it behind. An outcropping of volcanic rock was now between us and Fira. Glancing across the sea, we noticed birds flying below us along the caldera walls. It was amazing to watch them catch the thermals and glide effortlessly below. We sat silently enjoying the view.

We looked down the path towards Oia. We could see that the trail would now move away from the buildings. The hike along the caldera would be in more of a natural setting and offer views of the rugged terrain. Cacti appeared along the path. It felt like an adventure in the making and the view seemed to spur Sara's enthusiasm. I too was ready to continue the journey; however I noticed a small grocery store off the corner of the parking lot. I thought we might need to get some snacks since we didn't know what other options we had between here and Oia.

"Sara, do you need anything, a soda or something? It might be a while before there's somewhere else to stop."

Sara shrugged. "I'm good. We still have some water. Besides, the people at the hotel told me there's a small food stand up ahead."

"Well, if you're good, let's keep moving."

"I think we have about another hour to the food stand and then another hour to finish. If you need some motivation, the food stand sells homemade brownies and wine."

I laughed. "You've done your homework."

The path took us down a steep grade. It seemed to propel us forward, though Sara's pace left no need for additional speed. I did enjoy the downhill section as we had been walking for the last hour. I could also see ahead that the path would move up several steep grades as the rim of the caldera was not flat by any standard. The rim was marked by jagged, volcanic peaks and valleys. The rugged terrain provided majestic scenery.

The silence resumed, but I accepted the fact that conversation wasn't needed to enjoy the hike and the brilliant views over the sea. I enjoyed plodding down the path and letting my eyes wander. It was serene and peaceful. I was feeling a sensation like an out-of-body experience. I felt like I was floating above, watching the two of us experience life. It was a surreal moment.

Ahead of me Sara paused. She was standing on a rock nearest one of the highest points of the trek. She gazed out over the water. I watched her scan the caldera rim from one side to the other. She appeared on top of the world and was quite literally on top of one of the volcanic peaks. I couldn't help but quietly slip out my camera and take a picture of her. It was a beautiful setting with a beautiful woman. On the screen of my camera, she was framed by the Greek scenery she had longed to enjoy.

As I approached her, she smiled and held out her hand. She motioned with her hand across the horizon. I smiled and without a word moved my eyes from left to right, following the path of her hand. It was breathtaking. It certainly left no doubt that leaving the ship had been the right decision. I'm sure both of us knew that we would never have experienced this hike and the accompanying views as passengers of the ship. I took a deep breath and shut my eyes. I opened them and scanned the horizon again. The colors were vibrant and everything in sight was highlighted by the sun.

To my surprise, I noticed that Sara had already started down the path. She was smiling and glancing back toward me, apparently wondering how long it would take me to notice she was gone. As my eyes met hers, she pointed toward the valley below. I could see a small food stand. There were a few tables next to it that invited weary hikers to stop for a rest. Sara was now about thirty yards ahead of me. The valley basin was only about five minutes away. I didn't try to catch up. I knew that we'd reunite at the food stand.

I continued at my own speed. In the distance I could see Sara approach the food stand and sit down at one of the available tables. I refocused on the scenery and felt a euphoric feeling throughout my body. It wasn't just the incredible views, it was the spontaneity and sense of adventure. Sara and I were in Santorini. Nothing else seemed to matter.

As I approached the food stand I saw Sara waiting for me under a blue wooden awning. The food stand was about the size of a shed, but the weathered structure and its white plastic chairs were a welcome sight. The potted red geraniums brightened the barren area and complemented the white and yellow wildflowers scattered across the rocky terrain.

Sara's smile was almost as big as the brownie she had on the table in front of her. She seemed to be waiting for my reaction.

I set my daypack on the table. "That's the most inviting brownie I've ever seen. Is it for the two of us or do I need to get my own?"

It was Sara's turn to laugh. "We can share. I think there's enough for both of us. It may be big, but I did pass on the wine. I figure we can wait until the end of our hike for a celebratory toast." Since we usually don't pass on an opportunity to have wine and we usually avoid brownies on a regular basis, I approved her choices. "I think there's enough of this incredible brownie to split and I can wait on the wine. We can share the water that I've been hauling along in my daypack."

Sara divided the over-sized brownie and I pulled out a bottle of water. She placed half the brownie in front of me and kept the other half. I set the water between us to share. Our simple feast was prepared.

I dug out the binoculars from the pack and laid them near Sara. "I've been carrying these. You might as well use them."

She immediately grasped them and held them up to her eyes, peering back along our path. "This is amazing. You can follow the trail all the way along the caldera until it turns to Fira. We've come a long way." Her smile reflected a sense of pride and accomplishment.

"Oh, I can see the snow-covered peaks of Crete."

I took a bite of the brownie and immediately lost interest in the setting. "Sara, you need to taste this brownie. It's still warm."

"I will! The woman inside the stand said they were fresh out of the oven," Sara replied, moving the treat toward her mouth. She agreed that the brownie was sheer heaven. In fact, I wasn't sure how heaven could be any better than the what we were experiencing at that moment. The view of the white-capped peaks of Crete, the shimmering sea, the rugged caldera cliffs, and a delicious brownie made this a heavenly moment.

We munched on our brownie and took an occasional sip of water to wash down the rich chocolaty taste. Our bodies seemed to sink into the chairs and our eyes were still fixed on the view. There was a peacefulness that overcame us. The silence had set in again, yet there were no ill feelings between us. It was more of a relaxed feeling that did not need to be interrupted. It was as if we both knew the scenery was meant to be enjoyed in silence.

During this time, I was thinking about whether I should check in on Sara and her concerns. It felt awkward thinking about breaking the silence, though it was hard to suppress the urge to say something. I truly wanted to assist her if she had any issues or needs, but I didn't want to ruin the moment. I probably seemed a bit squeamish as I adjusted my sitting position a few times.

Sara glanced at me. "You seem ready to go."

"I'm not in a hurry...whenever you're ready."

"The brownie's gone. We should move on before we stiffen up." She stood and stretched. "This was nice. Just sitting there with nothing more to do than enjoy the view and the taste of that brownie. It was perfect."

I ignored my calming thoughts. Before I could reconsider my urge to speak, the words seemed to jump off my tongue. "Do you want to talk about what was bothering you last night?" I immediately wanted to kick myself for asking.

Sara effortlessly pushed her chair toward the table and calmly looked in my direction. Our eyes really didn't meet. She appeared to look past me rather than directly at me. She responded softly, "Let's not. We have a hike to finish and I want to enjoy it. Let's just enjoy the hike!" She moved abruptly away from the table and started towards the hiking trail.

I felt a sinking feeling inside. I wasn't sure it was because she didn't want to discuss whatever it was or that she didn't invite me to assist her. In an apologetic tone, I called to her, "Sara, I only want to help you, if you need it."

She paused and looked back at me. Her smile was rigid. "I promise I will ask you to help me if I need you. Right now I wouldn't know what to ask for. Remember, we said we were going to leave all our issues behind." I nodded my head in agreement.

She looked directly into my eyes. "Just trust me, Jay."

She turned with a determined focus and walked briskly past the sign that indicated the direction of Oia. I followed like a dog that had been kicked by its owner, though the pain felt as if it had been self-inflicted. There was definitely a different kind of silence now.

The hiking route moved off the trail and along a road, making it necessary to walk a couple hundred yards on the pavement. It was a good excuse for me to lag behind and stay in single file so that we avoided any issues with passing traffic or between us.

As I peered across the road I could see water only a short distance away. To my surprise, this was the narrowest part of the island and you could easily see both the west and east coasts as they bordered the sea only a few hundred meters away in each direction. I paused, as did Sara ahead of me, but I still kept my distance.

It was a unique sight. On one side of the road the east coast stretched towards Kamari and across the other side behind us, the west shoreline circled back towards Fira. The coasts were dramatically different. The east was a flat patchwork of farmland that seemed to flow endlessly along the sea. The west was a rugged cliff that was more like a fortress meant to keep others from reaching the island.

Soon the path headed upward away from the road. It was the most rugged terrain we'd encountered today. The path itself was narrow and worn. One could only imagine who had followed this path over the centuries. Looking up the mountainside, I could see that the rugged land was terraced. The leveled land appeared to be too rough for farming. Perhaps it was an early effort to stop erosion? We were left wondering about the purpose of these small, rocky terraces.

This history-rich environment brought many tourists to the island. In the last decade alone, tens of thousands of tourists must have made this particular trek, all following this path which now moved in a northwestern direction and all seeking the beauty of Oia.

The gruff sound of rocky soil beneath our feet was the only noise that accompanied us on this part of the hike. The silence now seemed deafening. Sara continued her trek in a determined fashion and my thoughts shifted between our current rift and my concerns for Sara. Her words, "trust me" were lodged in my head. We had been married for a long time and I was searching the archives of our long relationship trying to figure out another time she had said, "Trust me."

Relationships should be built on trust. We certainly had developed a solid sense of trust over the years, but what really was trust? What did it mean in a relationship? I understood there should be respect for each other. You should feel physically and emotionally safe with each other. Over the years of our marriage we shared our feelings openly and were supportive of each other. We seemed to know when to compromise. I never doubted that our relationship was built on trust; yet in this instance, Sara asking for my trust meant that she didn't want my involvement. That was difficult for me to understand.

It think Sara was asking me to respect her privacy, asking me to trust her. It was difficult not knowing the issue. I was grappling to understand the meaning of trust.

I kept searching in my mind for any time before in our relationship when Sara said "trust me." I sarcastically snickered to myself because the only instance that came to mind was when our children were young. We'd gotten up early one morning and loaded the kids in the car for a long drive to visit grandparents. As we were about an hour into the trip, it suddenly occurred to me that we hadn't turned off the coffee pot. I panicked thinking that our house could burn down. When I voiced my concerns, Sara thought about the hectic departure out our front door and responded that she remembered shutting off the coffee pot. Knowing how hectic things were when we were leaving and how many items needed to be loaded in the car, I was skeptical. After a brief discussion, Sara said, "Trust me,

I turned it off." Her response eased my mind and when we returned from the trip I saw that she was right. The coffee pot was off.

Now I'm sure there are other times in our relationship where we must have said "trust me" to each other, other than this trivial instance, but nothing came to mind. Yet if you asked me if there is trust between us, I would respond, "without a doubt."

We trusted each other on many levels. We kept things confidential within our marriage. We set goals together and considered each other's interest and well-being. Our marriage came first. We had invested a lot of time in our relationship. All those simple moments we took to connect with each other helped ensure that we built a trust. We didn't play controlling games and didn't act with ulterior motives within our relationship. We truly wanted the best for each other. That's why not knowing what was bothering Sara was so troubling.

I tried to shrug off the silence. After all, the majority of our time on this hike was in silence, though I knew that this silence was very different. I was beginning to feel her concerns had nothing to do with the kid's separation. There seemed to be some greater concern, but for the moment, I was asked to be trusting. The silence continued to hover in the air.

I could hear Sara's breathing getting deeper, as she pushed herself to climb up the steep incline. Earlier in the hike the walkway meandered up and down through the village, but here the inclines were steeper and longer. Nonetheless, whatever goes up, must come down. I could see that once we reached the summit, we were going to be rewarded for this climb with a long downhill slope.

If Sara didn't know about the kids, I wondered what else was wrong; however, that brought some inner thoughts on trust in our relationship. If Sara said, "Trust me," shouldn't I just drop it and trust her? Shouldn't I focus more on the incredible hike along the coast? Maybe I was the one who had the trust issues since I was keeping something from her, though I kept telling myself that I was only supporting my son and his wishes to temporarily keep the news from his mother. The silent time along the trail seemed to engage my mind and I did little to restart the conversation between Sara and me.

We'd been together long enough to understand trust. We'd faced many challenges in life together and formed a special bond with each other. The challenges of raising three kids also added to that bond. You might think that family life would dull the intimate side of a relationship and it may in many couples, but we not only cherished the time we spent with our kids, we also cherished the time we had together. We always felt we were nurturing our relationship, sharing intimacy, and building trust.

I paused at the top of the incline. The sun was shining across the sea and the jagged cliffs dropped straight down to the water below. It was as if a beautiful painting hung before me. Though we had seen variations of this view for the last two hours, I was still amazed. It was like another masterpiece in a gallery filled with priceless art.

Sara was sitting on a large rock a few yards from me enjoying the masterpiece. Her eyes were fixed on the horizon. There was a contented smile on her face and a relaxed look to her body. She turned and smiled at me.

It was comforting. I moved to sit next to her. I could hear her breathing deeply and rhythmically. She appeared to be pulling every bit of oxygen out of the air, reinvigorating her body and enjoying her surroundings.

I could feel my own breathing deepen as I mimicked her breathing pattern. I felt in tune with her body as we breathed simultaneously, our eyes fixated on the sea below. I glanced up at her and said, "Sorry for asking."

There was a pause. Sara stood up and gave me a warm smile. "Just trust me." I offered her a reassuring smile and nod. She winked, turned, and continued down the path.

For the next half hour, I trailed behind Sara on the single footpath. There was an easing of tension and a more relaxed feeling in my stride. I assured myself that I did trust her. I also was wise enough to know that if she wanted to leave an issue aside, I should abide by her wishes. Silence was a powerful tool in our relationship. Though she had spoken only two words—"trust me"— the silence that followed the spoken word was emphasized.

Much of the time during this portion of the hike I focused on my son and the issues he and Kathy were dealing with. I thought about the day before we left on our vacation. He stopped by to return a pair of hedge trimmers. I could tell he was a bit down by the way he walked through the front door with his head lowered. His eyes appeared to be looking more at his shoes than at me. The spark that was usually apparent when he entered our home wasn't there.

He initiated some small talk about working up a sweat that afternoon and how he'd filled two large garbage cans with trimmings. He'd greeted his mother with a kiss, but within seconds he headed to the garage with the clippers. He'd called to me to join him so I could show him exactly where the clippers were stored. When I entered the garage, he stood silently, looking at me.

"What is it, Tommy?"

He looked directly at me, but hesitated to speak. I'm sure it was difficult to tell me about something he wasn't proud of or happy about. Finally, he blurted it out quickly. "Dad, Kathy and I are separated."

I was taken aback. My voice came out in a hushed whisper. "I'm sorry, son. What do you need?"

Two grown men in a garage usually exchange greetings and grab a beer from the old refrigerator; however, we both stood looking at each other. I was waiting for a response from him and probably not knowing where to start, he stood silently staring at the ground. The silence was broken when he reached out his arms. I didn't hesitate to embrace him. Being taller, he pulled me towards him and I could feel the hearty pats on my back. It felt more like he was consoling me.

"What happened?" I asked.

"I left the house," he replied, seeming relieved that he had confided in me.

Our conversation continued for about five minutes. He informed me that he was staying at a hotel for a couple of nights. He asked me about staying in our house while we were gone.

"Of course," I said. "Our home is your home."

As our conversation came to a close, he said, "Don't tell Mom. I don't want to wreck her vacation."

I looked at him and put one hand on his shoulder. "It's between you and me. If you need anything, you let me know." With that remark we both headed back into the house.

~~~

Sara neared the top of what was our last peak before we descended into Oia. There was a small Greek church with the classic blue dome perched on the edge. The white buildings of Oia glazed the narrow tip of the island. It was as if someone had dipped a piece of chocolate biscotti in white chocolate. The white paint of the buildings vividly contrasted with the dark volcanic rock. We could see the path winding its way to Oia.

"Take my picture next to the church with Oia in the background," directed Sara in an upbeat tone.

I reached for the camera. "A good picture," I told her. I adjusted the zoom lens to capture Sara from the waist up, with the panoramic view of Oia in the background. I snapped the shot. It was magnificent.

Before I could share it with Sara, she was asking a German tourist if she would mind taking a picture of the two of us with the same background. I handed the camera to the friendly bystander and positioned myself at Sara's side. I reached around her body and this time I placed my hand on her hip. She reached for my other hand. We put our heads together and smiled. I could immediately tell by the way our bodies touched that all was well. I trusted it was.

We were about to descend into Oia. We had hiked along the rolling trail enduring the ups and downs for nearly three hours. Most of the hike was done in silence on the narrow, single-lane path. There was silence as we enjoyed the majestic views along the caldera. There was silence that provoked thought. There was silence that signified tension. There was silence that brought us together. Silence appeared to be an important factor in our communication.

And after all this time of silence, I was finishing the hike wishing that I had been more silent. I wished that I had never asked Sara about her worries. She asked me to trust her and I should have respected that request. My mind also focused on those powerful words: "Trust me."

I really didn't have much of an opportunity to talk to my son about the reason for the separation, but I wondered what had happened between them. Were they able to build a level of trust in their young marriage? How could they understand the complexity of trust in a relationship when I still seemingly struggled with it after a long committed marriage? I pondered what I would advise if I had the chance to sit and talk with him.

We started the descent to Oia. I took a deep breath and enjoyed the experience in silence. Sara seemed to be picking up her pace again. The long hike appeared to have taken a bit of her swagger, but now that the end was in sight, she pressed on.

We passed a few caves along the route just outside of Oia. We were told by some other hikers that there was a luxury hotel with cave rooms. I was also surprised to see so many small resorts as we neared the village. They seemed very peaceful and offered beautiful caldera views and amazing sunsets, but I preferred the sea side location of Kamari.

We headed across an industrial-like parking lot and ventured down the path leading to the main road. The actual village was about another half mile up the road, but after a long hike, the bus stop ahead of us was inviting. I asked Sara, "Should we just catch the bus here?"

Sara paused briefly and then with a renewed sparkle in her eyes, she said, "We can catch the bus here, but let's wait in the little restaurant across the street."

Across the street was an archway leading to a wonderful courtyard with white walls and yellow tables. The sign indicated that it was the Anemomilos restaurant. Beyond the white walls with yellow accents was a beautiful courtyard.

Sara smiled. "I bet they have cold beer and some lunch."

"I like the way you think, wife of mine."

~~~

Across the road we marched with a determined stride. Within minutes we had an ice cold, 500ml bottle of Fix beer in front of us. The Greek salute of "*Yamas*" was quickly exchanged between us. The expression on both of our faces indicated that the first taste was refreshing and well deserved.

Sara was the first to speak. "That was an amazing hike. I'm so glad we decided to start this incredible adventure."

I tipped my glass toward her and we clinked glasses to celebrate our achievement. I took another swig of the frosty beer and added, "You can cross that one off your island bucket list. It really was amazing."

Sara didn't respond immediately. She appeared to be sinking into her chair, her head was tilted back and eyes nearly shut. I could feel my tired muscles relax too. The completion of the hike had brought on a sense of accomplishment. It was quiet. I shut my eyes and took a deep breath. I cleared my mind and enjoyed the silence. I trusted all was well.

Chapter 9
Pyrgos Perspective

Two people can look at the same thing and see it differently. Our perspective can be formed by our past, our interests, and our outlook on life. It is important in a relationship to consider things from our partner's perspective.

Spyros, the owner of The Boathouse, had just dropped us off in the main square of Pyrgos, which was the highest village on the island and the capital of the island in the early 1800s. We both paused to examine the matrix of winding stairs that climbed steeply up the face of the village. Above we could see the Kasteli Castle, one of five Venetian castles built on the island in the 15th century. The hilltop landmark marks one of the highest points on the island. In fact, only the monastery on Mount Profitias Elias may be higher. We were promised that the view would be worth the climb.

However, our legs were a bit worn out from yesterday's six-mile trek from Fira to Oia. Sara had slept through breakfast. I'd slipped out of the room quietly and joined the other guests for breakfast. While I enjoyed the conversation with the international group, Sara seemed to embrace the opportunity for additional sleep.

Having only a chance to grab a cup of coffee as we departed the hotel, she was still a bit sluggish. Her enthusiasm for hiking had been much greater yesterday. Today her mood seemed less adventurous; however, this jaunt was much shorter and less strenuous. The village itself was unique in that above the main square there were no streets, only the narrow, winding walkways originally constructed to confuse invaders. We were told that there were many fortified walls and hidden passages within the village. From our perspective in the square, it appeared to be one large labyrinth.

Since Sara appeared tired, I knew it was not the best time to discuss anything about her apparent concerns. She had told me to trust her and I would. I felt our relationship had a strong foundation built on trust and I would have to rely on faith that all was well. Despite wanting to know more and to ensure that everything really was fine, I knew I had to move on and be upbeat.

We followed a path that led to the first flight of stairs. A quick glance from the bottom of the steps to the castle at the top indicated that there was no straight up route. In fact, it was difficult to see any route within the walkways that made its way to the highest point in the village.

"It's is going to take a while to find our way to the top," I said. I was ready to conquer the climb.

"We have all day," responded Sara. "We can take our time and look at some of the shops."

I noted her lack of enthusiasm for climbing the stairs and agreed. As we started upward on the first flight of stairs, Sara insisted, "We need to stop for some food somewhere. I need more than a cup of coffee for breakfast."

The winding stairs were literally a maze. The buildings and waist high walls did not allow you to veer from one walkway to another. We quickly determined that if you made a wrong turn, you needed to retrace your steps and find another route. It appeared that the main public walkways were outlined in faded white paint. Those that were not painted led to private residential areas. Upon this realization, I began surveying the pathways for the quickest route upward.

Sara rolled her eyes and laughed. "Don't worry about the destination, just enjoy the journey."

I chuckled and realized that I needed to back off and relax a bit more. Throughout our relationship I had always been the one determined to get to our destination in the shortest amount of time. On the other hand, Sara was more likely to stop and view the sights along the way. There were countless times during our family travels that we passed signs that said, "Lookout Ahead." If I was driving, I routinely would point at the sight as we flew by at seventy miles per hour. If Sara was driving, she would pull over and open the car doors for the kids to get out and enjoy the sights.

There was a famous event in family history during a cross country car trip to visit grandparents in which Sara was driving and I fell asleep. A sign on the highway indicated that the Corn Palace in Mitchell, South Dakota was only twenty miles away. This site interested Sara and the kids and knowing that I was asleep; they took advantage of the opportunity to take the exit. I awoke outside the Corn Palace and soon found myself in an old gym filled with murals made of corn. It was not my idea of a worthwhile stop and it had added forty miles to our journey. I think Sara and the kids enjoyed the corn murals more because of my grumblings. To this day, the recollection of this story brings a laugh from my adult children, but they all can say that they have seen the Corn Palace in Mitchell, South Dakota.

Knowing that Sara wanted to proceed at a slower pace today, I held her hand and together we moved up the steps. The whitewashed, mid-18th century steps were worn. They were not spaced evenly, which made them a little more difficult to navigate. As we walked, I sensed the history beneath us. The Greek warriors who defended this fortress or even pirates who once invaded the village, had traveled these same winding, uneven steps. If only their worn edges could tell the stories of all those who had passed.

Sara again reminded me that she was in need of food soon. It was late morning, so an early lunch was in order. The narrow stairways did not allow us to see very far ahead and no restaurants were in our immediate view. Following the winding stairway for another couple hundred steps, we noticed a hand-painted sign on the walkway floor where the stairways split that said, "Kasteli Restaurant" with an arrow pointing to the left. We followed the path in that direction at a quickened pace in search of food.

There were a few small shops within this intricate maze of buildings, but Sara's intention of finding food apparently took precedent over her urge to shop. She glanced at some of the souvenirs and artwork displayed along the walkway. She politely declined the invitations of shop owners to check out their goods. She would flash a pleasant smile and respond, "Maybe a little later today."

I squeezed her hand. "Don't be so intent on the destination, take time to enjoy the journey," I teased.

Sara couldn't resist a smile and replied firmly, "Food is essential."

We continued up the meandering stairway and the crooked walkways of Pyrgos.

After a few more minutes, we saw another sign. It indicated that the restaurant was 100 meters ahead. A look of relief washed over Sara's face.

As we turned a corner, the weathered wooden door to the restaurant appeared in front of us. It was half open, leaving us to wonder if it was open for business. Sara pushed the door inward and peered inside. She was quickly greeted by the owner, who spotted her quizzical look and enthusiastically invited us into his restaurant. Sara responded with a wide smile and thanked him in Greek. I followed behind and also thanked him for his hospitality.

Sara was standing in front of me as if frozen in place. Her eyes were fixed on the horizon. The weathered door was the gateway to an open air restaurant with a view over the island landscape. The whole eastern side of the island lay across the horizon. We could see miles of Greek countryside rolling off the mountain base all the way to the glittering waters of the sea. It was breathtaking.

The owner motioned for us to take a prime table at the edge of the restaurant. We were the only ones in the small eatery and had the panoramic view all to ourselves. We both expressed our appreciation for the table and marveled at the patchwork of land that lay below our perch. Our hosts at the Boathouse were absolutely right—the hike up the stairs was certainly worth the effort.

"Wow!" was the first word out of my mouth.

Sara added, "This is remarkable."

The hike yesterday along the caldera certainly had provided incredible views, but this was different. Being in the highest village on the island provided us with a totally different perspective.

Trying to stick to our healthy regimen, we ordered a Greek salad and a glass of wine. The freshness of the ingredients always made this standard order a sure thing. Sara enjoyed the large piece of feta cheese that always topped the salad. For me, being up earlier and already having enjoyed breakfast, the wine was more appealing.

Sara surveyed the view. I watched her eyes scan from one side to the other. She paused, took a deep breath, and asked me, "What do you see?"

I chuckled at what I considered to be a trick question. I answered, "I see fields with roads running across them. I also see houses by some of the fields and clusters of houses that make up the villages. I see the sea surrounding the land." Without pausing, I returned the question, "Now tell me what you see."

Sara paused for a second and appeared to collect her thoughts. "I see a palette of colors. There are dozens of shades of green, blended with yellows and framed by the blues of the water. The mix of soil colors are endless. To me it is more of an abstract painting featuring various geometric shapes. It's a work of art." I knew she really did see the view from a more artistic perspective than I did. I'm definitely a concrete realist; she's an artistic free spirit, yet our different perspectives seemed to complement each other, rather than create conflict.

I nodded to acknowledge Sara's interpretation of the landscape and to show my appreciation of her perspective.

Without warning, thoughts of Tommy and Kathy sneaked into my mind. They both had their careers. There were times when they seemed very close and other times when we could tell that they were edgy towards one another. They had different careers, as well as varied interests and talents, but don't all people? How do some people turn differences into complementing features? Why do people let differences create conflict? It was an important question for our kids or for any other relationship. Why did this all seem so easy for us?

Our glasses of wine arrived with our salad and we quickly toasted. Sara was ready to get food into her stomach. As she munched on her first bites of cucumber and olive, I paused to re-examine the view. I could see the palette of colors she was referring to, but I was sure my eyes weren't seeing it in the quite the same way she did.

Sara, we see so many things so differently."

She nodded. "You sit here and see a network of roads. Your eyes follow them to familiar destinations and to locations where we could go. I'm not saying that you don't see the beauty in the view, but I focus on the colors, shapes, plants, and the overall beauty first."

"You don't notice the roads or try to find familiar sights in the land below?" I asked.

Sara quickly provided more insight. "I do, but I just pause and take in the artistic side first. I will say it again, you are more about the destination and I am more about the journey."

I didn't know if I should admit that she was right or be upset because she didn't give me enough credit for enjoying life. I had to ask. "Do you think I rush through life without enjoying the things around me?"

Sara seemed ready to reply. "I don't think you rush through life—you're just goal-oriented and you do what it takes to reach a goal. I think you tend to look at things for a reason instead of enjoying them for what they are. You've had a great career and provided our family with many things as a result; however, I think because of our relationship, you have learned to look at things from a different perspective. You learned to enjoy different aspects of life because of me."

I nodded in agreement. "I do tend to agree with that. I also think that your life has been better because I helped you reach your goals."

"Without a doubt," she responded and then added, "Our relationship as a couple has benefitted from us being our individual selves. We've learned from each other and adjusted our perspective on life because of it. I think marriage may be more about complementing differences than similarities."

"I find that interesting. I guess everybody is unique and we have to learn to love the uniqueness we all possess."

Sara looked at me as if she was in deep thought. She seemed to start talking with her mind still churning hard to process what was just said. She added, "Take it one step further. We're not only all unique and different, we're always changing."

"Oh, now that is heavy!" I said, laughing. "You mean to tell me that we not only adjust to our partner, but we have to be continually adjusting? No wonder people have trouble staying together."

Again, the kids entered my mind. If they went to counseling, could that enable them to see things from each other's perspective? It was difficult to assess since I didn't know the particulars of their separation. The thought of counseling and learning to look at things from the other's perspective seemed to provide some hope that they could work things out. Yet the harsh reality of the situation might be that if they had trouble adjusting so early in their marriage, would they be able to adjust further as their lives progressed? Maybe a successful relationship or marriage wasn't that easy of an equation.

I pondered the thought for a moment and again questioned myself why our relationship had been so successful. Then, as I was about to say something, Sara said, "Would we be here if I hadn't had the idea of leaving the ship?"

That brought a laugh and a full admission, "No, I will give you 100% credit for that decision."

Sara found that humorous, but added, "You did leave the ship without much hesitation. Had you been on your own, you would have thought about the repercussions of leaving rather than the benefits."

I quickly defended myself. "I'd call them responsibilities, not repercussions."

Sara agreed. "Yes, but your focus would not have been on the adventure."

I nodded in return because I knew she was right. If it weren't for Sara's insistence to leave the ship, I wouldn't have been on this adventure. I knew that before I left the ship I would have arranged for lodging, re-booked airfare, and contacted home to make sure Tommy could watch the house for an additional week. It was the way I approached things and my perspective on life.

The restaurant owner interrupted our conversation. He inquired if everything was okay and if we needed another glass of wine. We assured him the salad was wonderful and we wisely declined another glass of wine. When we complimented the view, he told us that we should take a path along the Kasteli Castle that climbs even higher and provides a view of a greater portion of the island. He also shared more information on how the castle was built as a fortified settlement to protect villagers from pirates and invaders. We thanked him as we rose to depart and provided a generous tip for his hospitality.

We'd had an insightful conversation. I'm not sure if we complicated the equation to a successful relationship or provided some important insight. The view was worth the stop and we'd had a very relaxing lunch. I appreciated Sara and her perspective and certainly felt that she appreciated me and mine. Though we were different, we were somehow stronger together. I also felt that our kids could develop the same type of relationship. Knowing that they were seeking counseling gave me a bit of hope for their marriage. Talking things through could provide a shift in their perspective of each other.

~~~

We followed the directions to the trailhead, which was very near the restaurant. The journey along the side of the castle on a narrow, cracked walkway gave us some unique views of some of the residential areas. Within the simple whitewashed homes of the village there were also some more elaborate, upgraded homes. Many had pools and decks overlooking this remarkable view. From our earlier perspective in the square, the front side of the village was very traditional and looked like it had remained the same for hundreds of years. However, by looking off the opposite side of the village, we could see that many of the residences had been modernized. It definitely was a different perspective.

The walkway ended and as the restaurant owner indicated, a worn dirt pathway led upward along the outer castle wall. We followed it about 100 yards until we reached the pinnacle. The panoramic view included much of the island and enabled us to see the incredibly diverse landscape. There was farmland, mountains, beaches, and the caldera, captured within a single vista under the sunny skies of Santorini.

"Let's sit and enjoy this," I suggested. Sara grinned and sat down without hesitation. We snuggled together and scanned the horizon in silence. I may have been trying to locate the various villages on the island and Sara may have been examining the landscape shapes, but it didn't matter. We were both enjoying the view.

Sara was the first to interrupt our viewing. "I'd ask you what you see, but it really doesn't matter. You just have to enjoy the view for what it is."

I simply responded, "Thanks for pulling me off that ship."

She immediately leaned over, put her arm around me and kissed me. I returned the kiss. As I did, I realized that it was the first time I'd really thanked her for insisting that we leave the ship. I also realized that for most of the last hour I had set aside all my thoughts about home responsibilities. Even the concerns Sara had expressed and the thoughts about our son and his wife seemed to be vanishing. We were alone on a secluded ledge behind an ancient castle enjoying one of the most beautiful panoramic views in the world.

We had found a corner of the island that few tourists have on their agenda. We certainly would not have had the time to venture to this dirt path alongside one of the highest buildings on the island during the brief stop on the cruise tour itinerary. This is the type of exploration we'd dreamed about. We'd taken time to venture beyond the main tourist areas.

The longer we were in this spot, the more relaxed we both seemed to be. It was a very peaceful moment.

I pointed to the caldera rim and remarked to Sara that Oia was the far point on the island. The cluster of white buildings made it easy to locate. Sara remarked, "That was a long, but beautiful walk. I will always remember that."

A warm smile moved across Sara's face. "This whole trip will be one of our greatest memories. Santorini will always be our special place."

I put my arm around Sara's shoulder and gave her a tender hug. "Time has stopped and we're the only ones in the world right now."

"It seems that way. It's good that it's just the two of us," she said, looking directly into my eyes. "When we sit here, do you see us as a couple or as individuals?"

I chuckled before responding. "Are we back to exploring our relationship?" Before Sara could answer, I added, "I think that's a simple answer. It's simple math.

The integer of one plus another integer of one equals two. So we are two individuals that make a couple."

She moaned. "Now that's romantic. You have this beautiful panoramic view and a romantic setting and you quote me a math equation. We have different perspectives of this moment."

I laughed and confessed that I knew that answer would get her to respond with a bit of emotion. "Oh honey, I knew you were looking at this as a romantic couple moment that brought us together, but I wanted to put a bit of a realist twist on it."

"I don't know if I appreciate your humor at the moment, but there's some value to your perspective, though I was reflecting more on our other conversations about our relationship. Here we are sitting on rocks behind an ancient castle enjoying the moment. It's that simple thing, we don't need anything fancy."

I responded sincerely. "Sara, it's also a few moments where we take time to connect with each other. We've been together the whole morning, but this moment is a time together away from everything. Sometimes I think that we do it so often that it's just part of our daily routine."

She appreciated my insight. "It's all that and more."

"More?" I questioned.

"Yes. We're exploring the island and taking time to look further into our relationship. I do value the time we connect, but, in reality, your math equation does fit. We are two individuals that make a couple. We see things so differently and have so many different interests, yet we enjoy so many things together."

"People are like snowflakes, no two are the same. Aren't all couples two individuals who together make a couple?" I asked rather bluntly.

Sara didn't hesitate to respond. "Then why do we feel our relationship is so strong and other relationships don't succeed? Why aren't we 2-1=1?"

I smiled and responded, "You are very sexy when you get mathematical."

"Oh stop it," Sara said giggling.

She pointed across the landscape. "Do you see the piece of land out there that looks like a lion with a big mane?"

I scanned across the horizon surveying the different shapes made by the plots of land below. It took a few seconds, but then I responded with enthusiasm, "Over there, where the road makes a big round turn and the brown field borders the tan colored one. The rock piles look like eyes."

Sara was surprised. "You do see it! More importantly, you see what I see."

Puzzled, I said, "Of course I see what you see."

"No, we don't see the same thing. Remember, you said people were like snowflakes. We see things differently, from different perspectives. You didn't see the lion until I pointed it out, but what mattered to me was that you saw what I saw."

Not fully understanding her point, I said, "Give me credit for seeing the lion."

"Stop and think," Sara said, holding her hand out like a school crossing guard halting a row of cars. "Don't say anything else," she instructed. "We are two completely different people. We have different perspectives on many things, but right now your perspective changed because you listened to my perspective. You were willing to look at the landscape from my point of view. Think about our relationship. It's strong because we know we're different, but are willing to look at things from the other's perspective. We don't dig our heels into the ground. We do value the other's perspective. We compromise. We're willing to look from the other person's perspective."

I nodded several times, pausing to think about what she'd said. I looked at Sara knowing she had a valid point, but I needed clarification. "I have to ask...what if I wouldn't have seen the lion in the landscape?" Maybe I knew the answer, but I had to ask.

Sara said, "I would have helped you find it. I would have shared the clues that I'd seen. I would have taken your arm and pointed to the area. Maybe I would have described the roads since that's how you view the landscape. We would have worked together for both of us to see it."

Inside I knew she would have. I sensed the emotion in her voice and saw that her eyes were watery. I knew she valued our relationship and our perspectives. "You would have, Sara. I know you would have helped me. In fact, I know that you would have helped me find it and not criticized me for not seeing it. I really do know that."

Sara dabbed her eyes. "If you're keeping a list, seeing things from the other person's perspective is important in our relationship."

Trying to add a bit of humor to the moment, I said, "Now Sara, you don't think I'd be such a realist that I'd have to keep a list to analyze our relationship."

She appreciated the humor. "It wouldn't surprise me, but I'd understand."

We both chuckled and leaned forward for a hug.

Our time on the lookout point had come to an end. We stood up, preparing to begin the journey back. Sara lifted her t-shirt as if to flash me. Though she only revealed an industrial-strength jogging bra as her intent was to allow air to cool her body, I winked at her.

She turned to go down the narrow path first. I followed and put my outreached hand on her right shoulder. Her hand patted mine and I felt the appreciation of our discussion in her soft touch. We didn't say much to each other as we negotiated the path downward. Sara was more concerned with her footwork than furthering our discussion. A slip down the steep slope could negatively alter the enjoyment of our adventure.

The other structure that highlighted the village was the church, Agia Nikolaos. It probably wasn't considered massive by European standards, but was definitely large for this small village. Its large blue dome and symmetrical bell tower, both topped with a cross, stood like a sentry above the village. Before driving us up, Spyros had told us about how the village of Pyrgos and the church were very important parts of the Greek Easter celebration. His descriptions were vivid, explaining that on Holy Friday, referred to as "Big Friday" in Greece, services at the church are highlighted by setting the village a blaze, not by setting fire to everything, but rather filling hundreds of large coffee cans with sand and oil and placing them alongside every building in the village. When the thousands of cans were lighted, the blaze could be seen for miles.

He explained that this signals to the world that those who are Greek Orthodox are proud of their faith.

Inasmuch as Easter is the most important and cherished event on the Greek Orthodox calendar, the Pyrgos flames are a source of pride. Diane had shared some pictures from the Internet showing the entire city glowing with orange flames.

Now we were standing at the front door of the church. The steeple above proudly displayed five bells. The series of white arches gave access to the entrance. From its prominent location in the village, we could see down to the square where we had started. You could still make out the various features of much of the island.

"Can you imagine how far away you could see the flames at Easter?" I asked Sara, knowing that she was there when Spyros and Diane were sharing the information.

"You must be able to see it from Oia," she said, knowing that Oia was on the far end of the island.

"I wonder if you could see the glow from Crete?" I pondered.

"I wouldn't doubt it," said Sara. "If they wanted others to see the flames, I'm sure Pyrgos was the perfect place for allies and enemies of the past to see it from a distance. People from other islands should definitely be able to see it."

"Well, put Greek Easter on our bucket list. We might have to come back some day to see it ourselves."

"Whew! I like that you're already thinking of other trips. Your free spirit is developing, Jay!"

We took some time to look in the church. Acknowledging the fact that it's a religious building, we were very respectful. Sara took time to examine the statues and paintings from an artistic standpoint. I circulated through the church at a much quicker pace. I appreciated the tranquil setting and the reverence of the inside, but having gone to church six times a week as a Catholic grade school student, I was ready to exit quickly. I left Sara carefully examining a painting and told her I'd meet her outside on the front steps.

I didn't mind waiting for her. I knew she was in her element and she needed time to explore. To me, sitting on the steps, watching the people wander by while I surveyed the beautiful view across the horizon was time well spent. Today was very relaxing and our conversation had brought Sara and me together. I was going to trust her and not bother her about her earlier concerns.

I pondered what she'd said about us being two distinct individuals with different interests, but also being a very happy couple. I didn't think that the old adage "opposites attract" was especially true. Sara and I had many common elements between us. We were both from large families; we made our own family a priority. Being from the Midwest, we liked the outdoors, and we both seemed to adore each other. Yet, she loved movies and I didn't; she was enthralled by art, while I had only a passing appreciation; she read continuously, while I liked to spend time on the golf course; she liked pictures on the wall in unbalanced arrangements, while I liked them in rows of uniform frames. The thought brought a smile to my face, but somehow I knew it was the common things we shared and our willingness to accept each other that made us an inseparable couple. I wished the same for my son and though I promised not to say anything to Sara, I still found it difficult to keep this information from her.

Deep in thought, I felt a hand tug at the back of my hair. "Are you dazing out? I'm done inside," remarked Sara waiting for me to get up.

"Just enjoying the view and the peacefulness," I replied, rising to my feet.

Sara leaned over and gave me a big hug. "Thanks for waiting. I know I take longer to go through sites than you do."

"That's who you are and I love the whole you," I said with a smile, knowing that she'd appreciate a cheerful greeting after taking an extra twenty minutes in the church.

"We should head back to the square below. It's about time for Spyros to pick us up," I said.

"We shouldn't keep him waiting. He was so nice to volunteer to drop us off and pick us up. I really appreciate how helpful he's been," Sara added.

"He's great. He knows so much about the island which has really added to our trip."

"Without a doubt."

~~~

We started down the path, but we'd gone about thirty yards when we stopped and looked at each other. "This isn't the way we came up, is it?" Sara looked confused.

"Nope," I replied, chuckling. "I think we'll just have to weave our way through the maze. It has to be downward. I guess we should have dropped breadcrumbs so we wouldn't get lost in this Greek labyrinth."

"Just as long as we keep going down and don't run into any minotaurs, we should be fine," Sara added with subtle humor.

We wound our way down the stairs. Our strides appeared to be more like limping because of the uneven steps. We paused at each intersection and debated which way to go. It seemed like whichever path turned down, that's the path we chose; however, with the height of the surrounding buildings, it was difficult to see if we were heading in the right direction. We laughed at each dead end and pondered our choice at each fork in the path. Our mood was whimsical and we were enjoying the adventure of the maze-like stairs and pathways.

About twenty minutes later, we reached the road at the base of the village. The sights were unrecognizable, but that only evoked more laughter. By looking at the village landmarks above us, we decided we needed to head in the direction that took us up the road.

We'd guessed correctly because after walking about 200 yards, we could see the town square where Spyros was going to pick us up. I put my arm around Sara and we walked side by side. It had been a wonderful visit to Pyrgos. We'd enjoyed the day and made light of our navigational skills through the village.

From my perspective, Sara and I had again connected. We'd delved into our relationship and explored a corner of the island off the beaten path. Everything in life seemed great. But then again, perception doesn't always match reality.

Chapter 10

Red Beach Beauty

All relationships should embrace spontaneity. We should not dwell on what we have missed in life, but focus on what life has to offer. Spontaneous relationships enjoy laughter, romance, passion, and fun.

The bright, rust-colored sand of Red Beach lay along a crescent-shaped bay a few hundred yards below us, its rugged features giving more of an appearance of Mars than Greece. Our legs were weary and our spirits hesitant to pursue another day of hiking. We'd decided we needed a day of leisure and after a conversation with Evie at breakfast, we made a spontaneous decision to travel to Red Beach. A beach day might be just what we needed.

The sea breeze was cool on our faces and fluttered Sara's hair and she pushed it away from her eyes. The moist air felt refreshing. The white waves of the sea washed ashore below, as if giving the beach a fresh coat of paint. The deep red of the wet sand contrasted with the lighter shades of dry sand. A few people scurried along the water's edge, while others bathed in the sun. The array of colors—swimsuits, towels, and umbrellas, were vivid against the earthy backdrop. Two white sailboats, spotlighted by the sun, skimmed across the water in front of the beach. Their movements were effortless and peaceful, much like us at the moment.

Evie had shared with us that Red Beach was the most well-known beach on the island of Santorini. It was neither the largest, nor the most accessible, but it was known for its rugged beauty. The rich red sand and the rough, jagged cliffs suddenly gave way to the blue Aegean waters.

We could have stayed on Kamari beach right in front of the Boathouse Hotel, but we wanted to explore every corner of the island. Red Beach sounded like it needed to be on our itinerary. We had to take a crowded bus to the southwest side of the island, but standing on the ledge looking out over the beach made the effort seem worthwhile.

The path from the parking lot winds a quarter mile back and forth up to a spot that overlooks the beach and then continues down a more challenging, rocky path to the beach itself. In fact, it appeared most of the tourists who ventured to the lookout point decided not to walk the extra hundred yards on the steep, fairly treacherous path to enjoy the beach. A steady stream of people moved between the parking lot and the lookout point and viewed the beach from above. Many just spent their time buying jewelry and fruit from the local vendors who displayed their wares along the trail.

Sara and I held each other and posed with big smiles while a woman took the picture of us perched high above the beach. Her husband offered a bit of framing advice, though I thought with this background there was no way she could take a bad picture. I doubt that the real beauty of this place can be captured in a photograph. Two clicks and our camera was handed back to us. The woman smiled and asked Sara, "Are you on the Norwegian cruise?"

I couldn't help but grin and turn toward the beach with my back to them. It might have seemed rude, but I didn't want them to see my smart-ass grin.

Sara replied, "No, we're staying in Kamari. We love it there."

The woman looked a bit surprised. To avoid a prolonged conversation, Sara quickly added, "Thanks for taking the picture. We're going to hike down to the beach."

The husband grabbed his wife's hand. "Have fun, we need to get back to our tour bus."

They started back to the bus and we focused on the path leading toward the beach.

"I'm so glad we don't have to rush to the tour bus or return to the ship," Sara said.

"I agree, but while we're eating cheese and crackers for dinner, they'll be dining on steak and lobster, and their choice of two desserts!"

Sara chuckled. "I know cruises are decadent, but my dream was to explore this island. Just think of all we've done in just a few days."

I put my hand on her shoulder. "We made the right choice for us. Now let's head to the beach."

The minimal hike down to the beach went well, except for Sara's issue with heights. She's fine when she's on solid ground and a safe distance from the edge, but this path had a base of loose rock and rickety handrails. A misstep could have serious consequences.

"Sara, are you ready to venture on down to the beach?"

She replied a bit hesitantly, "Yes, I think so. I don't want to pass on this opportunity."

"I'll go first and you can put your hand on my shoulder. Just let me know if you need any extra help."

Trying to show that she was overcoming her fear and appreciating that I offered to go first, she teased, "Good, I can look at your butt."

I chuckled. "Are you insinuating that I was looking at your butt on our earlier hikes?"

Giggling, she replied, "I know you were. I could feel your eyes."

There was no further argument from me. I adore Sara. I appreciate her beauty and love her adventurous spirit. We've kept our relationship fresh all these years. It was intriguing to me to consider the questions of "why" and "how." In fact, it was probably more intriguing when I pondered what I added to the relationship.

~~~

The path was about two feet wide. The loose gravel made it a bit difficult to negotiate between sharp, volcanic rocks. We didn't try to go too fast. Instead, we moved patiently between each protruding rock. After a couple of minutes of cautiously placing our steps, the path dropped steeply between extremely large boulders. There were two sets of wooden railings made of weathered two-by-fours. They didn't look very sturdy, but did assist us with balance. I walked about two steps ahead of Sara to guide her and provide a lending hand. She gripped the rough rail with one hand and pressed her other hand against the huge boulder on the other side. She intently watched her feet move slowly to secure her footing with each step. I kept moving downward in front of her. Sara's progress was steady and relief was visible on her face when she completed this part of the trail.

The next section edged its way along the side of a cliff that had no rails or ropes to support hikers. Sara turned her back to the drop off and moved sideways. She virtually hugged the rock wall, placing both hands on the wall and sliding one foot down the path, then following with the other, her toes practically scraping the rocky cliff face. The edge of the path was very loose gravel and with a thirty to forty-foot drop below. Sara faced the rock wall and avoided looking down.

Her movements were stiff and her pace was slow, but I happily greeted her when she hit firmer ground. The lower part of the path wound its way to the beach and was less difficult than the higher sections and Sara easily made her way. Though I am sure it seemed longer to Sara, we'd made our way down from the lookout point to the beach in just under five minutes.

"I'm down," exclaimed Sara, as her feet hit the red sand of the beach. "That wasn't so bad."

We both turned and focused on the beach. There were plenty of sunbathers and walkers crisscrossing between the water and the rocky cliffs. The sand beneath our feet appeared to be a mixture of fine black and rust-colored sand. An impressive red catamaran glided into the harbor. It appeared to be a sightseeing cruise with about twenty passengers aboard. The white sails arched against the pale blue sky. There were only a couple of puffy clouds that dotted the horizon like pieces of floating cotton. Bright spots of fluorescent red and yellow could be seen as kayakers paddled through the sun-lit waters. Two small islands, their bleak colors fading in the distance, served as a backdrop to this incredible picture.

We observed a velvety soft layer of moss and dried vegetation scattered across the sand as we walked toward the beach. Our feet sank like we were walking on sponges. The gray substance appeared to be a type of seaweed that had collected in this area. We tiptoed across it for twenty yards.

Our eyes not only scanned the busy beach in search of a place to lay out our towels, but also scoured the sheer cliffs that rose above. The rough texture of the walls appeared to be like a sturdy, rust-colored natural stucco.

Also catching our attention was a series of old weathered doors that were built into the side of the cliffs. There were about five of them, each two to three feet off the ground. They had an eerie feel to them. Evie had told us that they were doors to boathouses that fisherman used in the past, but today they're used more for storing beach umbrellas and chairs that are rented to tourists during the high season.

As I examined one of the weathered, wooden doors, Sara flipped her towel and started to stake out an area for sunbathing.

The doors hung on large wooden beams that were secured into the rock wall. I tugged on one of the massive doors, but it was locked. I could only imagine what type of cave was behind the aged wooden planks.

After trying my luck with the cliff face doors, I turned and plopped down on the towel Sara had laid out for me on one of the only vacant areas on this side of the beach. She was already sitting on her towel, with a bottle of sun screen between us, gazing out over the sea.

"There's another party boat pulling into the bay," she reported, holding her hand up to shield her eyes from the sun.

"I saw that there are boats that sail out of a town called Perissa. They advertise trips to Red Beach," I reported. I'd seen the signs at the Fira bus station.

"Maybe we're too old for that type of excursion," said Sara.

"Too old!" I exclaimed. "We'd be the life of the party!"

"Probably too old," Sara said with a grin. "We could check into a sunset cruise."

"We're not too old. We have too much fun to think about being old."

"You may not want to admit it, but most of the kids on that boat would consider us geezers."

Laughing, I replied, "In that case, I think I'll take my old geezer nap."

Sara laughed. I laid back on the towel and peered up into the clear sky. I could see rocks sitting on the cliff overhang above us. They weren't swaying in the wind, but nearly half of each rock, at least eighty feet above us, was visible.

"We should maybe think about moving away from the cliff walls. There are some dangerous-looking rocks on the edge of the cliff above us."

Sara glanced upward and responded, "They've been up there for centuries. I think we're safe."

No sooner had she said that when a few tiny pebbles tumbled from the ledge above and landed on our towels. We both stared for a moment in silence before I said, "I think we need to move away from this area."

Sara nodded. "No arguments from me. Maybe that's why this spot was empty."

We grabbed our towels and other belongings and walked farther down the beach. The center area was crowded, so we opted to move toward the far end. We felt that was a wise choice, not only because there were fewer people, but because the cliffs weren't as high, nor were they as steep.

As we made our way between the beach goers, many of whom were younger couples, Sara remarked, "Wouldn't it be great if Tommy and Kathy could take a getaway and spend some time here?"

"It would be," I replied, noting sounds of alarm and hesitation in my voice.

"They really loved their honeymoon in Cancun. I think my favorite picture of them is standing on the beach, holding each other. They looked so happy and relaxed...so much in love," said Sara, smiling at the memory.

I agreed with Sara and purposely responded with only a few words. "Someday they'll have more time for vacationing."

I waited to see if my comment would trigger a response from Sara to provide more information about the kids.

When she added, "It would be better sooner than later," I wondered if she knew.

Sara finally found a spot that was safe and also appealed to her. She moved toward an old slab of cement that was planted in the sand and slanted upward. She laid her towel along the base and leaned up against the slab, supporting her neck with my small tote. "This is perfect," she said, adjusting her body for comfort.

I smiled and laid my towel on the sand next to her. Her bright yellow bikini complemented her body and spirit. It was a good color on her and captured her positive outlook on life.

As we settled in, other beach goers arrived and settled near us. Since the hike down required proper footwear, most were dressed more for the hike than the beach. There was little hesitation for many of them to discreetly change from t-shirt and shorts into their swimsuits on the beach. In fact, the two girls nearest us wrapped a towel around their bodies and effortlessly slipped into a swimsuit bottom, placing their tops on the sand next to them. It seemed a bit out of the ordinary to this American male, but apparently was normal for a beautiful beach in Greece.

"How warm do you think the water is?" Sara asked with a smile.

Since I knew where her thoughts were heading, I started to get up. "I'll check for you, but I doubt it'll be as warm as you'd like." This was a regular occurrence for a visit to a beach or pool. Sara always wanted warm water above 82 degrees and since there usually wasn't a thermometer available, I was the water tester. I really didn't mind and like today, it usually was best if one of us stayed to watch over our belongings.

"I'll take the plunge," I said, bravely heading to the water. The dark sand absorbed the sun's rays, scorching the soles of my feet. I quickened my pace as I attempted to sprint the rest of the way as I sought relief in the water.

My entrance into the gentle waves was slowed by the small rocks that had collected along a ridge between the sand and water; however, I was able to stand on the rounded pebbles and feel relief in the cool water. The soles of my feet were soothed, but the small rocks pressing into my tender skin was painful.

The water was refreshing, though I assumed it was under Sara's minimum temperature requirements. After two steps into deeper water, I could see that the sea bottom was lined with large, rounded boulders, most about twelve inches in diameter. I gingerly stepped on the first of the many larger rocks and then another. On the third step, I plunged head first into the sea. Instantly, I felt a cool sensation and welcomed the weightlessness of the saltwater.

I glanced back at Sara, who I could see was watching my reactions. Even though the water was a fraction cooler than what I would have liked, I calmly waded and bobbed in the sea to indicate to her that the water was wonderful. Instead of heading back to the beach, I swam out farther and frolicked for at least five minutes.

Deciding to rejoin Sara, I swam to shore on my belly until I could no longer keep afloat above the rocks. I stood up, but needed to carefully negotiate the large, slick rocks below me. I intently watched my feet move from one to the next while bracing for the next wave to roll in behind me.

My eyes focused on my feet moving from the large rocks to the bank of pebbles. I felt more like a fire walker moving across hot coals. I attempted to move my feet in a gingerly manner, keeping my balance, ignoring the pain from the sharp edges, and moving forward as quickly as possible. The last step onto the warm, volcanic sand was a welcome relief.

Once both of my feet were firmly on the beach, I glanced in Sara's direction. She was sitting on her towel. Her knees were pulled up toward her chest. As I refocused to get a better view of her, she pushed her feet out, stretching her legs out straight in front of her. That brought a smile to my face because with her knees out of the way, I could see that Sara was wearing a beaming smile, but was topless.

"How's the water?" she asked, as if purposely redirecting the conversation away from her lack of beach attire.

"The water's great—a bit chilly, but certainly refreshing." I quickly added, "It should be a perfect temperature for a mermaid."

She smiled. "So, you don't mind?"

"No, I don't mind. I actually like your spontaneity."

She blushed a bit. "It's not like I'm the only woman on the beach without a top. Besides, I'm in Greece and this is part of the experience."

"You don't have to defend yourself, honey. You look beautiful and I'm glad you're relaxed and confident enough to do it."

"Thanks! I didn't know if you'd be possessive or upset," she giggled, "although I did think you might enjoy the view."

Obviously, she knows me well.

"Is the water really warm enough?" she asked in a more serious tone.

"It is. It feels a little cool at first, but you'll adjust quickly. The buoyancy is great."

"Then I think I'll go for a dip."

"Be careful of the rocks on the bottom," I warned. "You may even want to wear your flip flops in."

Sara reached for her top and looped the strap over her head. She tied the strings around her back and started toward the water. I watched her tiptoe quickly across the hot sand. Just as I did, she stopped at the sea's edge to allow the cool water to soothe her feet. She appeared to handle the rocks well and was soon bobbing with each wave. Sara always enjoyed being in the water and this seemed to be the relaxing day she needed.

She dove under with her arms stretched out, her legs straight and toes pointed as she disappeared under the surface. I watched as the water rippled and her head popped up about five feet farther from shore. She laid back and let the waves roll under her. Her slender body bobbed up with each cresting wave, floating in her own carefree world.

A large sailboat with another load of partiers glided into the bay about forty yards beyond where Sara was swimming. About twenty people were on deck dancing and holding red Solo beverage cups, likely filled with a cold alcoholic drink. No one seemed to notice, or care, that someone was swimming nearby.

Watching Sara made me grin. I thoroughly enjoyed observing her in her present state—playful and lost in her own little world. She was enjoying all that Red Beach had to offer.

The grin on my face kicked my mind into gear. I felt our marriage was one that encouraged spontaneous fun. We wanted to get the most out of life. We cherished the times that brought out the inner child in us, allowing us to simply enjoy ourselves. In short, we both knew that life had many responsibilities, but we also knew we shouldn't take it too seriously. Life was meant to be fun!

My mind also wandered to Tommy and Kathy again. They were young professionals embarking on their new careers. They seemed to have limited time to be together. Being in your twenties can seem like there's a mountain called "life" standing in front of you, challenging you to climb it. Though I reminded myself that they didn't have kids, which I often falsely equated to having spare time, I knew they were a busy couple. I wondered how they found time to connect. Were they spontaneous? Though I couldn't manage their lives, I hoped that they'd noticed how we lived our lives. As a parent, I wondered what we could do for them at this point, and I felt a kind of sinking feeling in my stomach.

Suddenly there was a quick reboot in my system as I glanced toward the sea. There was Sara walking across the beach. She pushed her hair behind her shoulders. The sun was glistening off her tan body, as the water beaded like tiny crystals on the surface of her skin. Her bright yellow bikini clung to her body, accentuating her figure. After thirty-five years, she still caught my eye.

"That was heaven," she said, picking up her towel to dry herself.

"You looked like you were enjoying it. You're the most beautiful woman on this beach," I said sincerely.

"Yeah, right. I'm almost sixty years old and you think I'm the prettiest babe on the beach. You'd better get new contacts."

"Well, in my opinion, you are."

"That's great, Jay, but I think I'd trade bodies with a couple of the girls over there," she said, motioning to four girls on a blanket just down the beach, all with perky, tan breasts.

"I won't complain about the neighbors," I said with a smile, "but you were the Red Beach beauty floating with the waves."

Sara smirked. "Thanks, glad you think so."

It was my turn to sit up, as Sara laid down on her stomach to dry off in the sun. To my surprise, she untied her bikini top, slid it off, and put it beside her before resting her head on her forearms.

"Do you want to talk about our relationship?"

"You are really getting into this exploration of our relationship, aren't you? You never cease to amaze me."

"Well, I had time to think while I watched you swim in the sea."

"And what were you thinking?"

"I think we have a lot of fun together and we're spontaneous."

"Do you think I'm too spontaneous sunning without my top?"

"Hell no! I think you're enjoying the moment. I think there have been a lot of times in our marriage when we just have fun. We do some spontaneous stuff, but nothing too outrageous. I think we know how to have fun together."

Sara popped up, supporting herself with her forearms. She gave me slight smile. "Where would our relationship be without spontaneity?"

"On a cruise ship!" I quickly responded, triggering a chorus of laughter from both of us. "You're spontaneous, Sara. You're always amazing me—jumping ship, climbing mountains, casually casting off your bikini top."

"Men are so easily amused, but I do think that couples need to have fun to keep a spark in their relationship. There isn't a script for marriage or life. I think when it starts feeling like you're following a script, you need to mix it up."

"I see where you're going with this, but it's a double-edged sword. Many people would take that to mean looking outside their relationship to seek other things or other people to mix it up with."

Sara pushed herself to an upright sitting position, exposing the faded, white triangular patches on her breasts.

"It's fun moving away from the script, but you have to be genuine. You should express your true feelings and be open to new experiences together. My insistence to leave the ship could have easily resulted in an argument instead of an adventure."

"I guess it could have. Spontaneity tends to decline the longer the relationship lasts. I hear a lot of people complaining that their spouse is boring and they don't do anything fun. That's definitely not us—never has been."

"You're right! We keep it fresh and definitely have fun doing it, though I think we put a conscience effort into it," Sara added.

"Remember how I bought you flowers every month for like the first five years of our marriage?"

"You were so romantic."

"Romantic, yes, but I'd never get them for a special day or event. I always brought them home when they were least expected. I didn't want to bring them on the 3rd Friday of every month or when you'd expect them. I didn't bring them on your birthday because you'd expect them every birthday. I brought them to you sporadically. I got you other gifts on your birthday, anniversaries, Valentine's Day, whatever, but I wanted to be spontaneous through the entire year. I wanted you to appreciate the surprise of the flowers. I wanted to have fun giving them to you. It was playful."

Sara grasped my hand and smiled. "I loved receiving them. I felt like a princess who had a very charming prince."

I knew she appreciated my efforts. In fact, I know she felt a bit spoiled at times because her friends' husbands would forget anniversaries and birthdays, while she often received surprise gifts.

"Play a game with me." Sara ran her fingers through her hair. "It will help define how we've kept our relationship fresh, spontaneous, and fun."

"Count me in, but first I need a quick dip in the sea. This sand heats things up and the cliff behind us cuts some of the wind. I'll be right back."

"Okay, I'll take another plunge when you get back," she called after me as I headed toward the water.

I moved briskly toward the water, glancing at the nearby blanket covered with young, beautiful girls sunning them-selves like mermaids. Though they were pleasing to the eye, I couldn't resist glancing at my own mermaid, who waved in my direction.

This time I spent only a couple of minutes in the water, just long enough to dunk my head and cool my body. The comment that Sara made about the kids and the spark on their honeymoon was true. I wondered why things fizzled so quickly. Sometimes they appear to take life too seriously. I could visualize their honeymoon picture on the shelf in our family room and the eyes of my son telling me that he had separated from his wife. Both were etched in my mind.

As I was returning to my towel, Sara was heading toward the water. Without hesitation, we shared a hug as we passed. I gave her a quick kiss on the cheek and a pat on her behind. "Enjoy!"

I watched Sara plunge into the water with a graceful dive, much like she had done earlier. After all these years, I still marveled at her. Though I may have glanced at the topless girls down the beach, there was never any doubt that Sara was the woman for me. Our relationship was solid. We'd kept it fresh and playful. We seemed to pull the most out of life. It was not a cliché, it was a reality. As proof, here we were on an unscheduled stop in Santorini.

Sara returned to her beach towel. She quickly patted herself dry and spread the towel on the sand.

"Are you ready to play my game?"

"Sure! Just explain the rules."

"We each need to think of three things we've done as a couple throughout our life together that have kept our relationship fresh. Not one-time things, but general things that we've done on a regular basis."

"You're talking about things that are spontaneous or fun—stuff we do often."

"Things that help keep our relationship from becoming stale, stuck on script...boooring!"

"Okay, then what?" I asked, waiting to hear the rules for Sara's game.

"We'll take turns sharing the word and then we will see if we agree with each other. You can add a sentence or two to clarify your word," Sara added with a devilish grin.

"Alright, I can go first. I think I have the obvious one," I said, wanting to please her.

"Which would be what?"

"Wine." I smiled at her and Sara nodded. "Wine is for lovers. We have wine to complement a wonderful meal, to relax together. We share ideas over a glass of wine, we plan vacations, and sometimes we're just plain silly."

"I guess that's as obvious as it gets for us. You're so right. Wine brings us laughter and love. It pulls us away from our routine and gives us a chance to be together. I can't argue, wine is for lovers. Well played."

"Your turn!"

Sara seemed ready to respond. "Notes." I love our notes. You leave me notes by the coffeepot, I leave them for you by your shaving kit. I've found notes in my work lunch bag, you text cute messages. They're small things, but they send a strong message."

"They're fun. I appreciate the artwork on yours. They come out of nowhere, when you least expect them. They're spontaneous reminders of our love. That might sound dorky but they are."

"When I get one, I can't wait to get home that day," Sara gave me a mischievous smile.

"This is kind of fun, we do make an effort to mix it up. Here's a big one," I said, "Hotels!" During our entire time together we scheduled one-night stays—usually only a short distance from home. Those 'staycations' were really total getaways, like we were a million miles away."

"No doubt. They were short, but we stepped outside our routines and enjoyed our time together. It wasn't always easy finding babysitters, but I wouldn't trade those nights for anything."

"I guess this trip isn't our first escape from reality," I added with a chuckle.

Sara agreed. "Okay, my second one is 'Dance.'"

I grimaced. "At first I hated that one!"

"That's why it's my favorite. You had to go out of your comfort zone. I knew you did it just for me, so that's why it felt special. But you did learn to like it, right?"

"I did to a point, though it wasn't easy. But like anything, if you have a little bit of success, it becomes a little more enjoyable. I enjoy dancing with you and I'll admit, we do have fun dancing."

"And romantic, I might add. Thanks again for taking all those classes."

"You definitely got me on that one." I thought for a few moments. "My third one is 'date night,' but not the ones where we went to the hotels. They were great, but I mean the date nights we had at home, the times we put the kids to bed early and had a nice meal on the patio. We knew we couldn't always leave overnight or take time to go out on the town, but we created a romantic setting at home."

"Good one! Our house could get a bit chaotic, especially when the kids were younger, but we found the calm within the storm and enjoyed every minute."

I laughed. "Not every minute. I remember the time when I brought the filet mignon off the grill into the house and Mary threw up at my feet. She was feeling sick and was coming to tell you."

"Oh, I'll never forget it. I guess we adjusted well to parenthood. Poor kid."

"We adjusted to a lot of things."

"Alright, my last one," said Sara. It's what we did pretty consistently. "Walking." I think our nightly walks were important."

"Yeah, a chance to stretch our legs and talk."

"It was time set aside for us. We walked for exercise, but really we enjoyed the chance to talk."

"It was enjoyable, but would you call it spontaneous?" I questioned.

"It mixed it up...got us out of the house. I know it was somewhat of a routine, but we didn't sit in front of the TV."

"I'm not sure that was spontaneous or fun, I'd call it enjoyable."

"That's why I wanted to look beyond one time things – not that you can't do something one time, but you have to keep enjoying each other. The walks helped us do that."

"No wonder we're happy after all these years. It certainly hasn't been the same experience each year. We've changed it up enough to make thirty-five years of different experiences."

"It has and it's been fun. Today is fun. Kind of back to that simple thing. Nothing too complicated, but we make the effort to enjoy whatever it is," Sara added thoughtfully.

"We do make the effort."

"We do, and it works."

~~~

The day at Red Beach continued. Our conversation was playful and reminiscent. We reminded each other of fun times during our relationship. We laughed at our spontaneous decisions in life and marveled at the fact that we were still in Greece.

We left the beach feeling like we'd gotten the most out of our day. We let the concerns of home and our regular routine drift aside. I really didn't want to draw any attention to our kid's separation. I didn't dwell on the fact that I was harboring a secret from Sara. Though I still sensed there was an issue she needed to share, I just totally enjoyed being with her, watching her frolic in the sea, totally relaxed on the beach, and adventurously sunning.

Today, like so many other times in our relationship, we left the script. We turned life in a different direction. I pushed our day on the beach into my memory, not because we did the expected, but because we spontaneously altered our plans. We chose to experience more in life.

Chapter 11
Orange to Black

To understand our partner, we need to listen. Listening is not just letting them speak, it's actively concentrating on what they have to say. Listen to their words; the inflection, the emotion, and the feeling within the words they speak. Listen with your eyes and your sense of touch. Listen carefully to the whole person.

In anticipation of a beautiful sunset, we returned to Oia. Our hike earlier in the week from Fira had taken us to the outer edge of the village where we'd caught the bus back to Kamari. We had only really seen Oia from the hills above, but we marveled at the narrow string of gleaming, white buildings along the sheer cliffs outward to the western edge of the island.

Now we were returning to enjoy its serenity in the evening. The narrow winding streets invited us to stroll at a leisurely pace. Surprisingly, Oia had an upscale feel to it. It blended the traditional Greek architecture with a cosmopolitan atmosphere. It was quieter than Fira, yet being perched on the caldera rim, it offered many of the same natural wonders to visitors. Known as an artists' haven, there were plenty of art galleries to capture Sara's attention. She wandered through many, as I reviewed an array of restaurant menus. The prices were higher than in Kamari, but we didn't just want dinner. We intended to find the perfect location to enjoy the sunset.

The main plaza in this tiered village centered on crossroads that were perfect for exploring this historic place. One side of the plaza boasted a large cathedral, its blue dome a focal point. Walkways branched out in many directions leading to quaint shops and restaurants. The caldera side provided a scenic view of the harbor far below. We watched a large passenger ferry and some small tour boats moving below across the gentle evening sea. This spot was one of the most photographed places on the island. We recognized the landmarks from the many ads we had come across in researching our trip to Greece.

As Sara read a plaque on the cathedral, my eyes focused on the view of the caldera. The sea crashed against the cliffs 200 yards below. I had an endless view of the water from the plaza. It was heavenly. Not being particularly religious, I was surprised by the inspirational feeling that came over me. I felt minute in this vast array of beauty. With a warm sensation on my skin and an appreciation for the view, I decided we should focus on finding a place to watch the sunset.

Soon we found ourselves in a second-story restaurant, sitting at a small table and once again looking out over the sea from the heights of the caldera rim which spanned the entire side of the island. Our eyes focused on the horizon, the sun high in the western sky. Our view was a mixture of blues and blacks, the sea and sky producing an amazing array of blues and the steep cliffs generating dark, rugged tones of black. The island of Thirassia lay just off the coast of

Santorini, cut away by the volcanic eruption centuries ago and now separated only by a narrow channel. Its jagged edges and barren landscape emanated a lifeless feeling. The black moonscape of its volcanic surface was only interrupted by a few white buildings of a small village on its nearest point. It left me wondering how anyone could survive on such a harsh piece of rock in the sea.

Yet this natural beauty of the sea and the landscape had drawn us to this northwestern edge of the island. We'd been told by many fellow travelers—and read in the guide books—that it would be a sunset we'd never forget. This was a popular destination. Since we wanted only the best seats for the experience, we'd arrived early. Our plans were to have dinner and enjoy our prime table until after sunset.

After taking an initial sip, Sara set her glass of wine on the table. "Mmmm...I love the local white wine. It's very crisp with a citrus taste."

"Delicious," I agreed after swishing the wine over my tongue. "It definitely pairs well with beautiful views."

"You think wine pairs well with just about everything." She gave me a smile and an eye roll before taking another sip. "It's good that we decided to get here about 90 minutes before sunset. Look at the people in line waiting for a table."

"Well, they won't be getting ours. We're going to relax and enjoy. I don't know how we could do anything else. It's exquisite."

Sara smiled and moved her chair slightly to the side as a couple was being seated at the table next to us. They thanked the waiter in English. I mouthed "English" to Sara, since we were surprised whenever we heard a

North American accent; however, we planned on enjoying the sunset as a couple and selfishly didn't want to start up a conversation.

It had been a very leisurely day. We'd slept in, but had made it down to breakfast before the 10 a.m. ending time. As usual, the atmosphere of the Boathouse Hotel had felt more like a family gathering in the courtyard than a normal hotel buffet. With only twenty rooms, everyone always seemed to strike up friendships. Even if there was a language barrier, guests always exchanged nods, smiles, and simple greetings.

The rest of our day had been spent on Kamari Beach. We rented a couple of lounge chairs and an umbrella. Our only interruption had been when we retreated to one of the beachside open air cabanas for lunch and enjoyed a couple of ice-cold local beers served by the restaurant's friendly beach cocktail server. She suggested we try a Yellow Donkey beer or a Red Donkey beer from the Santorini Brewery. We were thankful she did, as they were definitely some of the best beers we'd ever tasted.

It was another day of pure relaxation and the ice cold beer was nearly a necessity on the hot, black sand of Kamari. If heading to Oia to watch the sunset was the only adventurous thing on our itinerary for the day, we'd have to just enjoy it.

We were both scanning the menu trying to decide what would make our taste buds tingle. We also knew we were in no hurry for the food to come because we still had over an hour to wait until sunset.

"Sara, I think you should pick an appetizer, so then we can slowly sip our wine and put off dinner for a while."

"I won't argue with that. I'm already looking at the *dolmades*. Stuffed grape leaves would be a perfect match for this wine."

"I'm thinking of the grilled squid for an entree. You just can't get it as fresh anywhere else. We can be a bit indulgent since we have plenty of time to sit and enjoy."

"Yuck, those little tentacles gross me out, but you enjoy. I am going to have the moussaka. I hope they put a lot of cinnamon in theirs."

"Good choice, we can share a little bit."

"Wrong! You can keep your squid!" she said, her face crinkling in disgust. "But you can steal a little bit of mine."

Shortly after our food discussion, the waiter came to take our order. He was a handsome, dark-haired young man. He greeted us in excellent English and smiled broadly. We nodded in appreciation. Seemingly charmed by his welcoming smile, Sara started a conversation and inquired about the boats in the harbor.

"Are most of those boats below waiting for the sunset?"

"Every night the boats position themselves so their guests can enjoy our sunsets. We have the best sunset in Greece."

"There are lots of them. It must be popular."

"Yes. Like you, many people come to enjoy the sunset. Later you should maybe walk down to the harbor."

"You can walk down?"

"Only 291 easy steps," replied the waiter, eliciting a chorus of laughter from us.

"That's a bit much for an after dinner walk."

"Yes, I provided some comedy, but our harbor was once one of the main ports in Europe. In the late 19th and 20th centuries there were 150 ships in our harbor every day. Today tourists, but in the past, shipping."

"Do cruise ships stop here?"

"No, only the old port at Fira. We do have a passenger ferry that goes to a few islands."

Sara continued the conversation for a couple of minutes. The waiter told us that the early ship captains had built elegant houses on the highest points of Oia and that they were still there. He also shared that Greece still has the world's largest shipping industry.

After he left with our orders, we sat back and enjoyed the bread and olives, which had become a tradition during our evening meals.

I soon realized I'd forgotten to share a schedule change with Sara. "Oh, I almost forgot. I got an email from the airlines just before we left, our flight has been changed."

"What! When?"

"I don't think you'll have a problem with the change. We depart from Santorini one day later."

"Oh!" replied Sara, with a pause in her response.

It wasn't the reaction I'd expected. I'd really expected her to immediately react with excitement because we'd have another day on the island. Another day added to her dream trip. What could be more perfect for her?

"Oh," she said again and then she paused for a moment. "What about a room for the extra night?"

"No problem. Diane said she'd work it out. The worst case scenario is that we'd have to switch rooms, but she'll see what she can do." I certainly hoped that the reassurance would engender a little enthusiasm.

"Actually, that will be fine," she replied flatly. "I need to change an appointment, but that's no problem."

"Are you sure? What is it?"

"Nothing—you just caught me off guard."

Her response was still less exuberant than I expected, which struck me as odd. Hoping to add an incentive for the inconvenience it may have caused her, I injected, "Diane also invited us to her birthday party. She would have done it earlier, but thought we would have already checked out."

"Really? That sounds fun! She's so sweet."

"She'll let us know the details tonight or tomorrow. It sounds like a festive party."

Our conversation was interrupted by the couple next to us. The woman raised her voice so that most everyone could hear. "You never really listen to me!"

The man angrily relied, "Here we go again!"

Probably realizing that everyone could hear them, they reduced the volume and continued their gruff exchanges in hushed tones. We really couldn't hear the specifics, but then we really didn't want to. It was apparent that they weren't on the same page about something and their body language clearly signaled that they were upset with each other.

About two minutes later, the argument seemed to stop, though we felt another explosion could happen any time. We peered out of the corner of our eyes and could see that they were both leaning back in their chairs, red-faced and gazing away from each other. You could cut the tension with a knife. The waiter cautiously made his way over to their table and hesitantly inquired,

"Can I do anything to assist you? Maybe another glass of wine or more bread?"

There was no immediate response from either person. The man glared at his wife. She gave a one word response, "Whatever." Taking a deep breath, the man looked at the waiter, shook his head and replied in a dejected tone, "Just bring us the bill."

That was the last word exchanged between the couple. They both gazed at the setting sun without saying a word. The bill arrived, the man left cash for the waiter, and then they got up and walked briskly toward the exit. All eyes in the restaurant followed them.

I redirected my eyes toward Sara, "Wow! That opens a table for someone else to enjoy the sunset."

"Talk about a dream killer. They'll remember tonight, but for all the wrong reasons."

"What do you think it was?"

"Who knows? She evidently didn't feel that he listened to her."

I shook my head in disgust. "That's too bad. They didn't even finish their wine, let alone enjoy the Oia sunset."

"They should take a closer look at their relationship," Sara added with a bit of sarcasm.

Our appetizer arrived. The dolmathes, six rolled grape leaves stuffed with rice, glazed with olive oil, and garnished with yogurt, were a piece of art and they looked absolutely delicious. I was already finishing my first bite when Sara asked, "What does it mean to listen to someone? Obviously, it's not enough to just be quiet while someone is talking."

"I'm not defending him, but it does take two to tango. Beyond that, I think listening is a form of respect.

If you want to understand a person, you certainly have to listen...give them your undivided attention."

"Probably true and judging by that couple, if you don't feel someone is truly listening to you, there definitely will be problems."

"Yeah, but...Oh look! The pinks and reds are spreading across the sky."

"Oh Jay, this is going to be a beautiful sunset. I can't wait."

"It'll probably at least another forty minutes until it sets."

"Even better, more time to enjoy ourselves!" said Sara. "What were you going to say before?"

"Oh yeah, there are lots of types of listening. You can listen to learn, listen to understand, listen to yourself, listen to your intuition, on and on. I don't know if you can pinpoint one type of listening."

"That's the point, you have to always listen. The couple obviously had issues about listening to each other. I think listening is essential for any relationship."

"Do you think I listen to you?"

"I really do, we tend to talk things out. We listen carefully so we understand each other. For instance, I shared my dream to spend time here, you listened and here we are. That shows me you understand me."

"Or that I'm as crazy as you are!" I teased, but then quickly added, "I do try and I think I do understand you most of the time. We're both good communicators; however, I think you listen to everyone in the family better than I do. You're a compassionate listener. I think you get that from your mother. People like to share with you because they like how you listen."

The waiter arrived with our food. The squid was a large portion with many smaller tentacles surrounding the edge of the plate. The grill marks seared into the meat made my mouth water, but the look on Sara's face indicated that she wasn't interested in examining it too closely. Her moussaka was a layered mixture of potatoes, eggplant, beef, and spices. It smelled heavenly and judging from the aroma, it contained the proper amount of cinnamon that she loved. We nodded approvingly and welcomed the food.

Sara stared at the plentiful portion of food in front of her. "This will definitely keep us eating through the sunset."

"It will. I thought we'd be sipping wine slowly just to make it to sunset. This has been so wonderful, sitting here and talking."

"After seeing the other couple, I'd add sitting here and listening too. It appears listening is as important as talking, maybe more."

I chuckled, but couldn't help feeling bad for the departed twosome. "I guess you do have to listen to understand someone. Sometimes you need to set your feeling of "self" aside and give your partner your undivided attention."

It was Sara's turn to inject some humor, "You might have said that to the guy at the next table an hour earlier tonight. I feel bad for her."

"Well, if you don't listen to each other, what do you have? Not much. Just think, they couldn't even enjoy an evening in Oia set aside to watch the sunset. That's sad."

"I am not sure they'll be together much longer. If you don't think your partner is listening, you don't have a real dialogue."

Glancing toward the horizon, I could see the sun starting to drop toward the sea. "We'd better stop and let Nature speak to us with this amazing sight." We both paused and watched to the west. It seemed as if everyone around us had also stopped eating, taking the opportunity to watch this daily solar spectacle.

The vivid oyster pinks and rich earthy reds seemed to congregate above the water. As the sun lowered, pinks and reds gave way to oranges and yellows. As the seconds ticked by, the orange glare intensified as the sun hovered over the water on the horizon. The sky was ablaze and the water seemed engulfed by the burnt colors. I glanced at the black, rugged island across the harbor. The black volcanic rock was now a fiery orange. Instead of looking lifeless, it now seemed to burst with energy. Orange shadows were covering the white buildings of Oia, as if the earth had directed the sun to spotlight the village with an orange filter. The view was incredible. Everything within our sight was aglow.

I clasped Sara's hand. I didn't say a word for fear of interrupting this amazing experience. She squeezed back and a smile burst across her face, though her eyes never left the setting sun. The sky kept changing, giving way to the majestic red sun. For one moment, the sun hovered above the water, as if to take a bow for its spectacular performance, and then it dramatically disappeared.

There was some rumbling as people began to talk again. I watched the sky flicker with the last few fragments of peaceful colors. In an instant, the encore was over, Mother Nature turned off the lights to signal that the performance had ended.

I exhaled and glanced at Sara. Her eyelids seemed to have dropped with the sun. Her rhythmic breathing indicated that she had dozed off. She was relaxed and motionless.

"Sara," I whispered. Her head jerked up. "I think you dozed off."

"Meditating," she said. "It was so relaxing. It made my eyelids heavy. I've been so tired lately."

"Well, whatever it was, it was peaceful and beautiful."

"That was absolutely wonderful. That will forever be part of my Santorini dream," she said, rubbing her eyes.

"Now that was perfect." I smiled at my wife.

"I have never seen the sky so orange. If I painted a water color of that sunset, people would say it had too much orange in it."

"I know. I certainly don't think a photograph would do it justice either."

"Well, it's etched in my memory," said a very content Sara.

After nearly two hours at the restaurant, we still had food on our plates. No one else seemed to be in any hurry and the waiters encouraged us to stay and enjoy. The pace of dining was slow in Santorini and the setting sun only seemed to enhance the serene feeling.

"Was there anything else in your email?" asked Sara

"A bunch of junk mail and a couple of notices that our credit card statements were ready. Nothing urgent. I sent a note to Tommy to let him know that we'll arrive home a day later."

As if it were an afterthought, Sara added, "I saw I had an email from Kathy, but I didn't open it. I didn't have my reading glasses."

That sent a slight jolt of electricity through me. She said it so nonchalantly that it didn't appear that she knew anything about their separation; however, if she retrieved her reading glasses at the hotel and read the message, she may soon know the whole story. In order to leave the ball in her court, I responded, "I wonder what she wants."

Still savoring her moussaka, Sara added, "Not sure, but I'm glad she emailed me. It has been over two weeks since we talked. Hope she's doing okay. She seemed a bit tense before we left for the cruise."

"Really? Tommy was a bit tight too." I felt bad making the remark because it was like throwing out bait and waiting to see if she'd bite. The dilemma of not telling her as Tommy requested, still bothered me.

"They do get a bit tense with each other. They definitely aren't as bad as the couple that was sitting next to us, but I think they need to listen to each other more."

"Why do you say that?"

"They should pause and talk to each other more. I think they talk but, so much of it is in passing. They need to communicate more."

"If we're such good communicators, what would you tell them?"

"I'd tell them to make time for each other. Their relationship comes before work or anything else."

I was surprised by her comment. "Wow! That's direct. I guess I really didn't see the issues. You sound like you've mulled this over."

"Well, you told me I was a better listener and I'll confess that they both have shared some things with me."

"Really? What do you see as their issues?"

"Communication in general. They need to listen to each other more. Be in tune to each other. I can see it in their body language when things aren't quite right. They need to open their eyes and recognize it themselves."

"I know they're busy, and maybe I'm in a fantasyland, but they seem to be in love."

"Jay, I think they are. You know we've done a lot of things to keep our marriage going. Some of them we probably didn't even realize, but we always make time for each other. That creates the setting needed to communicate. The kids tend to come home from work at different times, the TV goes on, they each grab food out of the refrigerator or bring home take out and then they mess with their iPads for the rest of the evening. Do you think they're really listening to each other?"

"Welcome to the modern world. We had family meals probably because we had kids."

"And for the two of us, we had staycations, quiet time after the kids were in bed, coffee in the morning, and I could list more. Why are we good communicators? I think because we made time, we listened to each other, and above all, we were open and honest."

"I guess they have some work to do," I replied to the mother who had already assessed the kids' problems.

I pushed my empty plate to the center of the table, freshened my wine, and then reached over to pour some into Sara's glass. My hand motions were deliberate and slow, but my mind was spinning. The "open and honest" comment speared me in my heart. If I told her about the separation now, I'd be breaking a promise to my son; yet my inner soul told me to be truthful. I knew that if the news upset her, I would be there to support her. On the other hand, this was still her special time and she deserved it. At what point was I supposed to defy my son's wishes?

I finally replied, "It's more than time. That couple next to us tonight didn't communicate well, but they did have time together to watch the sunset."

"They didn't appear to listen openly. I'm not sure they wanted to listen to each other."

"You're right, it's not just time. You need to want to listen."

"I sense sometimes that Tommy and Kathy listen to the other to give themselves time for a rebuttal, not a solution. You have to admit that you've seen some of the tension between them."

"At times, but I guess I feel guilty because when I see it, we have them over for dinner or to an event and I think we're cramming one more thing into their busy schedule."

"We probably are, but we've always had a knack for balancing a busy schedule. We did it raising kids. We focused on the fun and prioritized important things. We laughed together. We didn't make it into an issue."

The waiter stopped by our table to remove some plates. We nodded in appreciation and realized how caught up in our conversation we were. He asked if we would like to enjoy complimentary Ouzo. Though we both looked in each other's eyes for approval, we decided against it. We expressed our appreciation for the offer and asked for the check.

"Sara, let's call it a night. We can continue our conversation under this beautiful moon."

I pulled her chair out and gave her a soft kiss on the neck. She smiled and though our conversation drifted from the sunset, we knew this was a magical night. It was truly an incredible feat of nature.

The soft glow of the village lights lit up the walkway along the white buildings. There were still quite a few people enjoying late dinners in the restaurants as we walked by. Everything was peaceful. A few owners invited us in to eat, but we respectfully declined. Hand-in-hand we walked toward the bus stop.

"Jay, you seem quiet now."

"My mind's on the kids. I didn't see the red flags."

"They were subtle, but I knew there were issues because they both shared some with me."

"That's because you're the better listener. You really care about people and talking with you has a calming effect."

"It may be part of being a good listener, but I am also the mom. That's part of it too. I think they'll be fine. I told them a lot of the same things I shared with you"

"I'm not sure it helped."

"Why do you say that?"

I stopped and turned toward her. Gripping both of her hands in mine, I confessed. "They separated just before we left on vacation."

"Oh no! You knew?"

I nodded my head in shame. "I did, because Tommy made me promise that I wouldn't tell you until we got home."

"Breaks my heart, I was so hoping they would work things out. It's so early in their marriage."

"Me too, not sure how things are going. I haven't heard anything from him on this trip."

Engulfed in the shadows of the buildings, we tightly embraced. I'm sure the sunken feeling inside me was only magnified within Sara. Over her shoulder, I could see the moon and the shimmering reflection on the water. It now appeared more distant and less magical. Reality had put up a barrier that hid the beauty of Oia.

Sara grimaced with a half-hearted smile, "I guess you blew that one by letting me know. I'm surprised Kathy didn't say anything to me. They must think you can handle the news. They look at you as the strong one."

"I'm not sure of that. They really wanted you to enjoy this vacation. Tommy only told me because he wanted to stay at our house."

"I'll read her email in the morning. You know a couple of minutes ago during the sunset, everything was full of energy, beautiful orange colors and peaceful, but now that darkness has fallen, it's black and feels kind of bleak."

"Remember, there are issues where we need to come together and support each other. This is one of them. The kids need to work on their relationship. We can't do it for them. We need to enjoy the last couple of days here."

Sara nodded in agreement, but said, "The parent in me wants the best for my son and I guess I can't always decide what's best."

Giving her another reassuring hug, I provided some additional information. "He said they're going to counseling. They're willing to talk with each other. Maybe an outside person will be able to get them to realize that they need to communicate and set time aside for themselves and their marriage."

Sara's watery eyes communicated her feelings. I knew the news was difficult for her to hear. I felt I had to be honest with her. As much as my son may not have wanted her to know, I knew communication was a cornerstone of our relationship.

There wasn't much talking about the kids on the bus ride home. In fact, we tried to focus our conversation on the incredible sunset and plan our activities for our remaining days. But, there was no denying that a cloud was hanging over us. Our spirits were dampened.

As the bus pulled into Kamari, a deflated Sara looked at me and said, "Marriage isn't simple, is it?"

Chapter 12
Tranquil Times

Honesty is the foundation of a good relationship. We trust our partner will be honest with us. However, we must realize that honesty starts with oneself. Understand that we can only communicate honestly with our partner, if we are first honest with ourselves.

It was time to jump off the bobbing water taxi. Holding her sandals in her hand, Sara leaped into the rolling water with a loud, childlike squeal. The splash into the knee high water sprayed back towards me. I immediately plunged in her direction, hoping to return the chilly spray. I tucked my beach tote under my arm and laughed as we splashed each other on our way back to shore. Our clothes were soaked and my wallet was a bit damp, but the playful departure from the boat was just what we needed.

The boat had just shuttled us from Kamari around the towering rock that separated Kamari Beach from Perissa Beach. The bus was an option, but it would have taken an hour to reach Perissa since a transfer in Fira was required. The boat was only four euros and took only fifteen minutes. It was our first chance to be on the water since we departed the tender boat nearly a week ago.

We'd had a restless night. Since Sara knew about Tommy and Kathy's separation, much of our conversation after returning to the hotel for the evening focused on them. Even though we both knew the separation was their issue and only they could fix it, it was an unsettling situation that disturbed our sleep.

We were both at breakfast early. For the most part, we kept to ourselves at a table on the far side of the pool. We had a chance to get a few details about Diane's birthday party. Spyros told us the party would be Saturday, which was only two days away. It would start at 2:00 p.m. in the Almira restaurant. It would be a family event, with a celebratory meal and some music. He also told us that most of the hotel would be filled with family members. It was something to look forward to and we appreciated his invitation. A celebration would help lift our spirits.

Sara read Kathy's email. Though she had her reading glasses on, she wasn't able to read between the lines. It simply read:

"I hope you're having a fantastic time. I can't wait to see you. I know we'll have plenty to talk about. Really do miss you! <3 Kathy"

It really didn't give her much insight because Kathy hadn't shared any information. It was clear to me that she was looking forward to speaking with Sara, but she also didn't want to interfere with our vacation.

Our time on the island was coming to an end. We had today and tomorrow on our own and then the party on Saturday. It was hard to think about leaving, but there was also a sense of being needed at home. Despite the interference of reality, we still had an urge to explore more of Santorini.

Yesterday, as we sunbathed on Kamari Beach, the cocktail server had told us that her favorite bar was Tranquility on Perissa Beach. She described it as a "trendy hippy bar with a New Age flair," which piqued our interest. She also said they had the most wonderful salads and comfortable lounging areas. She strongly encouraged us to visit and also shared information about the water taxi.

We knew from her directions that when we disembarked the water taxi, we would head down to the opposite end of the beach. As we began our trek, we felt a different vibe in Perissa than Kamari. It was a more laid back beach front. Kamari certainly had the romantic vibe, but Perissa was earthier.

The bars and restaurants appeared to be geared toward the younger crowd. They seemed to emphasize beach cocktails, lunches, and happy hours. Many establishments posted signs indicating that they maintained and serviced a section of the beach across the street.

We strolled toward the far end of the beach enjoying the new sights. It was a pleasant and much-needed distraction as we both wanted to let our minds focus on the moment rather than the issues with Tommy and Kathy.

Within a few minutes, we spotted the sign for the Tranquility Beach Bar. An overwhelming use of orange in the decor made it hard to miss. As we approached the front of the bar, we both started laughing.

Sara giggled. "This place was meant for us."

"Can you believe it? It couldn't be more perfect for the moment."

The sign above the entrance proclaimed in turquoise letters, "Live Life Simple."

At a time when we needed to enjoy a simple moment together, it was right in front of us. The hostess who saw our amusement greeted us.

"First time here?"

"Yes! And I think it will be perfect," exclaimed Sara glancing at me with a twinkle in her eye.

"We were told that you had the biggest and best salads on the island," I said as my eyes took in all the groovy decorations that left me feeling like I was back in the '60s.

"We absolutely do, you can sit anywhere in this section. Enjoy!"

We sat down on a couch made from shipping pallets. The wood was painted a glossy, bright yellow and was covered by vibrant orange cushions. This unique couch was extremely comfortable. The table in front of it was constructed from the same wooden material, only painted a brilliant purple. This place was not at a loss for creativity or colorful accents.

"Jay, I'd say this place is a cross between hippie and New Age. Did you see the sign for morning yoga classes?"

"I did, though while I was looking at the decorations, a waitress went by with a few salads that caught my attention."

"The one with the low cut top?"

"The salads, dear! You're funny!"

After only a short time in Perissa, our spirits were lifting or at least our focus was on having fun. It was good to laugh with Sara. Her laughter was music to my ears. I sensed this was going to be a laid back lunch, hoping it would provide a respite from any issues clouding our minds.

We ordered a half liter of white wine. We actually splurged and spent an extra euro to try the local organic variety. We then ordered a large cobb salad to split. After viewing the massive portions, we felt there was no way we could each finish one.

Our section of the restaurant was inside. Though it was covered, it had an open air feel. There were sections outside that provided additional seating with thatched umbrellas, a variety of furniture made from pallets, and even a fire pit. There was also a small stage area for live entertainment. This place positively created a relaxed and hip vibe. The logo of the bar was an impressionistic sun. It radiated the warmth of the welcoming hospitality.

Sara leaned back and curled her legs up on the thick cushioned couch. She gave me a look with those steel blue eyes which usually signaled that she was going to say something important.

"Thanks for telling me about Tommy and Kathy. It may not have been the perfect time to hear it, but it never would be. I'm just glad I know."

"Sorry to keep it from you. Tommy didn't want to ruin your trip."

"That couldn't ruin this trip. It weighs on my mind, but I keep telling myself it's something they will have to resolve."

"I do want them to resolve it. I love them both," I added.

"But if they're not happy, they shouldn't be together. I think the most encouraging thing is that they're going for counseling. If they're willing to explore their relationship, they might find that it is worth keeping."

I could resist asking a playful question. "Was the purpose of discussing our relationship so you could decide if I was worth keeping?"

"No, I think we are a 'thing.' I think it was more of a reaffirmation. It's a good thing to better understand our relationship."

"I think it's solid. No worries that I can see."

"I expect it is! Here comes our salad. See if you can keep your eyes on our food and not that cute thing with the cleavage."

"Here you go. One cobb salad. I had the chef split it for you," said the waitress swooping it onto our table.

"Oh my, they look good!" I said snickering, as the busty waitress set down the plates and departed.

"You're a funny one, Jay LaFavre."

"I'm honest and funny, my dear. And I can honestly say, I love you."

"Oh thanks, you're sweet."

As in many of the places we'd visited on the island, popular American-type music was in the background. We moved our bodies to the beat of the Bob Marley tune that filled the restaurant. The bartenders seemed to move with the rhythm and everyone around seemed to be bobbing their head or swaying with the music.

Sara, who always seems to know the words to every song, chimed in. "Rise up this mornin', smiled with the risin' sun...." With a playful slap on my shoulder, she continued, "Don' worry 'bout a thing, cause every little thing is goin' to be all right."

I watched with the biggest smile on my face. I clapped to the beat and watched her sing every word.

The song seemed to fit the moment. As she became more confident, her voice became a bit louder. It drew the attention of those around us and soon there was a small chorus of rhythmic clapping. Sara was the center of attention and enjoying every second.

As the song ended, her voice softly faded out. "Cause every little thing gonna be alright."

She acknowledged the polite applause and remarked, "I love to sing. It makes me feel so alive."

"You certainly looked like you enjoyed yourself. What an appropriate song."

"It was. I want every little thing to be all right and we have to follow the other half of that verse... "Don't worry! So we can't worry."

"Right on. We should enjoy the rest of our time. There's nothing we can do about the kids from here."

"Nor should we worry about anything else, so let's enjoy the salad and wine," said an upbeat Sara.

The next half hour was one of those times where we felt totally connected. We enjoyed the food and each other. We laughed, joking about living the simple life. We had fun; we drank wine, we laughed some more, we intently listened to each other. There were moments that I forgot we were in Greece. It all seemed so dream-like. We booked a cruise and by way of a spontaneous decision, we were here at a hippie, New Age beach bar in Perissa. I guess you can never predict where the path of life will lead you.

As we sipped the last of the wine, the waitress came our way. "Can I get you two lovebirds anything else?"

With a slight blush I replied, "No. It was excellent, but I do have one question. What's the charge to use the beach chairs?"

"No charge! Complimentary for our customers."

"Excellent!" I handed her the necessary euros to cover the bill, plus a tip.

The waitress added, "Do you mind if I send you to the beach with a couple of beers?"

"Not sure I need one," chirped Sara.

"They're complimentary," the waitress added.

"Really?"

"We usually give a shift drink to the employees and the lovely lady did a great job on that Marley tune. I think you deserve a couple on the house."

"Well, if I earned it, I'll take it," laughed Sara.

It seemed to be the perfect finish to a spectacular lunch. A cold beer on the beach, especially an earned one, was definitely in order. We grasped the mugs from the waitress as we headed out the door towards the beach.

The sun was shining brightly with a slight breeze blowing in from the sea. We crossed the road to a long string of brilliantly painted pallets that served as a walkway over the hot beach sand. The outlook on this day was brighter now that we both knew about the kids.

We ventured to a couple of chairs on the edge of the beach area designated for Tranquility customers. It provided some space to relax and a bit of privacy. We positioned the chairs under the umbrellas, since the sun's rays were intense. There was a small, circular table attached to the umbrella post to hold our beer.

"This day is just what we needed."

"It's perfect," laughed Sara.

"You're too easy to please."

"Lucky for you! Hey! On the serious side, was it tough not telling me about the kids?"

"Well, I wanted to tell you the whole time, but I also wanted you to enjoy this trip."

"Do I look like I'm enjoying myself? I just appreciate that you were honest with me."

"If I'd told you earlier in the trip, would you have suggested we jump ship?"

"Yes, without a doubt. Thinking of the kids would've troubled me, but I'm positive I would've insisted we leave the ship."

"That kind of surprises me. I really thought you would have wanted to go home early. It really churned my stomach keeping a secret from you."

"I still would've insisted on jumping ship!"

Her certainty was as reassuring as it was troubling. "Just when I think I know everything about you. You say something that seems so unexpected, but it didn't feel right keeping a secret."

"Honesty is part of who you are, Love. That's one of the things that keeps us strong."

"For the most part, I'm honest, but I'm not sure anyone can be honest all the time. Maybe that's why I grappled with it. I knew inside I needed to tell you, but I also made a promise to Tommy."

"Honesty and loyalty. I guess I see that as a difficult dilemma. I know that can be a challenge. Maybe there are times you feel you have to keep a secret or just avoid the truth to protect the people you care about."

"That makes me feel better, but I'll be up front with Tommy when we get home and let him know that I did tell you—at least it was near the end of the trip. That should make him feel better about it."

"It'll be fine. I think they'll both want some help or at least someone to talk to," Sara added.

"We'll offer advice, but like you said, they'll have to work it out."

"They will have to be honest with each other."

"Well, add honesty to the list of things that make a relationship work. Right now, I guess this tells me you have to be honest, even if it's hard," I added.

"I agree it's best to be truthful, but to what degree? I can really understand why you held off on telling me about the kids. You were protecting me."

"That doesn't make it right. If you're not truthful to your partner, you don't have much of a relationship. It should be the basis of any relationship."

Sara wanted to continue the conversation, "Actually, I feel you can't be intimate with each other unless you're honest."

"What do you mean?"

"Honesty isn't just about telling the truth. It's about being open with your feelings, being upfront with a person. It's expressing your true self in a relationship."

"You must have gotten an extra dose of Zen in your salad. Lots of hippie, New Age infusion there."

"You don't agree? How can you be intimate and have great sex if you don't express yourself openly? There's a whole spectrum to honesty in a relationship. You want great sex? Be totally open with yourself and your partner."

"Well, judging by our intimate ways, we must be pretty honest people," I said laughing. "But really, it goes back to living simply. Isn't it easier to be honest and open about who you are rather than being pretentious?"

"I'm not sure it's always pretentious. Maybe it's trying to protect the people you love. I agree that if you're not honest with yourself, you can't be honest with others."

Pulling our thoughts together, I gave my perspective. "You seem to be hitting on some good points. What I'm hearing is that if you're honest with yourself, you can then express yourself openly and truthfully and that allows you to grow as a couple."

"Oh Jay, that's a good cup of Zen."

"Am I right?"

"I'm not sure there's a right answer when it comes to relationships, but I think you pulled our conversation together pretty well. It's unquestionably important in any relationship."

Realizing how important honestly was, I looked at Sara and added, "We've been honest with each other for all these years and I'm sorry that I kept a secret from you."

"Don't beat yourself up for keeping Tommy's secret. I really do understand. I probably would have done the same thing," she replied.

We both glanced toward a group of chairs nearby. Six college-age kids were rearranging them to set up camp near us. We gave a discerning look to each other, but didn't object in any way. We were also too comfortable to move.

"I think they're from the U.S.," Sara whispered.

"Sounds like it. I heard one mention California."

Since I usually like to make friends on the beach and talk with people during our travels, I couldn't resist greeting them.

"Good afternoon, sounds like you're from the U.S."

There was an affirmative chorus and a lot of head nodding.

"Where are you from?"

There was a pause as they looked at each other, deciding who would speak first, and then they took turns sharing their own information. Two were on summer break from Stanford University, three were students at the University of Minnesota, and one was traveling by herself, just taking some time to sort out life. It turns out they all had met at a hostel only a few blocks from the beach.

"How's the hostel?"

One of the Stanford students replied, "Great! It's only ten euros a night and we have a pool, breakfast, and only four of us per room."

"Really?" I was surprised. "It sounds like some great amenities for that price."

Another shared, "We can sleep, eat breakfast, have one beer on the beach, and go to the mini mart for dinner stuff, all for about fifteen to twenty euros a day."

They seemed like great kids and I sensed they cautiously budgeted each euro they spent. Since the waitress had done a good deed for us and I had a soft spot for adventurous college students, I thought I should pass it on.

"Can I buy you a round of beers?"

Their eyes popped open and smiles appeared. They emphatically replied without hesitation, "Sure!" I glanced over at Sara. Her smile had turned into more of a laugh.

"Honestly, Jay, that's another reason I love you."

I signaled to the waitress to bring a round for our young friends. I requested Yellow Donkey beers, so they would have the opportunity to try the local beer. My new friends were thrilled with the selection and had no problem accepting a complimentary beer.

I was feeling better now that Sara knew about Tommy and Kathy's separation. A dash of honesty and a good deed on the beach had me feeling quite content. I also knew that we'd support each other in dealing with it and we'd do whatever was best for our son. Talking to our new neighbors also directed our conversation away from our relationship and centered it more on this adventure.

"What have you done while you have been on the island?" I asked.

"For the most part, we've only been here a couple of days, but yesterday we hiked to the chapel on Messa Vouno," chimed in one of the kids.

"Where's that?"

"It's the chapel built high up on the rock, that's Messa Vouno. There, up above Perissa," he said, pointing high above the village to a small chapel built into the side of the massive rock wall that separated Perissa and Kamari.

"You hiked up there? My knees would shake too much," exclaimed Sara.

Trying to ease her fears, the young lady of the group responded, "It's not bad, there's a well-traveled trail up there. It's the Chapel of Panagia Ketefiani. The villagers used to hide up there when intruders came ashore."

Another added, "You can take the trail and also hike all the way over to Kamari."

"How long does that take?" I asked.

"About two hours. I did it a little faster. At the top you can stop and tour Ancient Thira. It's an early Greek settlement."

"You guys have been good students and done your homework," injected Sara.

"Lots of time on our iPads—no TV at the hostel." This evoked laughter from all.

After a bit more discussion about the hiking, the beer arrived and our young friends were as happy as could be. They toasted us in unison, "*Yamas!*" We wished them well and sank back into our loungers. It was good to see such an adventurous crew traveling the world. There was just a slight twinge of jealously that we waited until we retired to venture to Europe.

The next couple of hours included more napping than sunbathing. The umbrellas provided some welcome shade and the chair cushions were comfortable. There was an occasional gesture from our friends, as they tipped their beers towards us to show how much they appreciated our hospitality, but they seemed to know that we were in our own relaxed zone. The cocktail waitress also made a few visits to offer additional refreshments, but we were content. The steady rolling sound of the waves washing ashore had lulled my mind and relaxed my body. The cool breeze wafting over my skin covered me in a blanket of tranquility.

Shuffling in her lounger, Sara sat up slowly. Her body indicated that she too had dozed off. She stretched her arms and then sitting sideways on her lounger, she moved her foot across the dark beach sand, apparently more focused on looking down and creating designs with her toes than enjoying the view. As she doodled with her toes, she resumed our previous conversation.

"You said you had trouble keeping Tommy's secret from me. Why do you think it was so difficult?"

"Like I said before, I don't like to lie to you."

"I believe that, but why was it difficult?"

I reflected momentarily. "The dilemma was that I didn't want to keep something from you and didn't want to break a promise with Tommy."

"But you didn't lie to me. You didn't say a thing. You didn't do anything dishonest."

"It felt like it. Even though I didn't say anything, I wasn't being honest with you."

"I think that fits into the spectrum of honesty that applies to all relationships. It's not just what we say, I guess it's what we're willing to share with each other," said Sara.

"I see where you're going. If we're honest, we have to be open with each other."

Pausing and appearing a bit uncomfortable, Sara asked, "So is anyone really honest all the time?"

"Well, if you want to be a pessimist, no. People tend to be honest most of the time, but not always. You also can't go through life expecting everyone is going to lie to you."

Sara seemed to be pondering the conversation. She looked out across the beach. "I think if you're honest with yourself, you'll express your true feelings better and be able to relate to your partner and others better. Though I understand, it's not always easy to do."

"I think you're right and there' a spectrum on honesty in a relationship. I can certainly attest that I harbored a guarded feeling every time the kids came up in our conversation. There was something hammering away inside me that kept me from opening up to you. Maybe my dilemma wasn't between my commitment to you or Tommy. The issue was with me. It didn't feel right to me. I wasn't honest with myself, let alone you."

"I agree. We need to be honest with ourselves first, and then we can express ourselves truthfully to each other but like I said before, you were just trying to protect me," Sara emphasized.

"Believe me, I think everyone knows when they're not being truthful. Maybe we tell ourselves it's okay not to be honest, but we know from the feeling inside us, something's wrong."

Looking at the ground, Sara added, "Saying nothing, not sharing your feelings or your thoughts—that's not being honest with yourself or with each other. I think it sounds easier than it is. I think that's an issue with Tommy and Kathy and a lot of other relationships."

"You're not saying that the kids lie or are dishonest with each other?"

"Not in the sense you're probably thinking, but if they fly past each other before work and after work, then they don't take the time to express their feelings to each other. They make great roommates, but they need to be honest with their feelings and let their relationship grow...be more intimate."

"I really sense that they do love each other."

"They do, no doubt, but a relationship shouldn't peak when they're newlyweds. They need to grow together. They need to better understand each other. The love is there, but it will flourish when they're honest with themselves and each other." Sara paused. "'Nuff of that, let's enjoy a few more minutes on this tranquil beach."

"We should. We're nearing the end of our time here. I'm gonna miss this place."

Sara didn't respond right away. Instead, she peered towards the ominous rock at the end of the beach. "So they call it Messa Vouno Rock. That's one large chunk of rock."

Sitting up and looking in her direction, I replied, "It's more like a mountain. It rises straight up from the sea like 450 yards high. It's unbelievable."

"That's the most unique chapel I've ever seen. It just sits on that ledge about halfway up the cliff. It looks so small from here."

"You see the path and the switchbacks going up. It looks easy to get up near it, but the path along the ledge may be a bit tricky. I can see why the people sought refuge up there."

"I think we've had enough rest today. I think we should hike up there tomorrow, maybe take the path back to Kamari."

"Are you kidding me? You're not great with heights."

"Did I not say that I wanted to explore every corner of this island? If it takes two hours to hike over, that's about half the time it took us to hike from Fira to Oia. I've lounged around most of the day. What else do we have to do tomorrow?"

"Let's put this in the context of our relationship discussion. I'll support your decision. You're certainly being spontaneous, but you have to honest with yourself. Do you really want to make that trek?"

"We didn't get here, on this island or in our relationship, by not reaching out for more in life. I don't want to get home and think about this day and say, 'we should have hiked to see the chapel or Ancient Thira.' We have only one day left and then Diane's party. Not much time."

"I understand. I'm just trying to make sure that you know what you are getting into. It's a pretty steep climb."

"Oh, Grasshopper, only half of the trip is steep. The other half is downhill."

"You are wise, my Greek goddess," I said, laughing at Sara's humor. "If that's what you want to do, I'll be right beside you."

Sara stood up and pulled her chair out from under the umbrella. She adjusted her beach towel and laid on her stomach, untied the back of her bikini top, and then grabbed her book. She glanced at me with a smile, "Before we hike tomorrow, we'll rest a little more today. I want to get some sun so I make sure I go home with a good tan."

"No problem. I could sit here for hours. This spot is so relaxing and calming. It couldn't have been a better day. It was just what we needed."

As my body relaxed and I adjusted the towel to support my neck, I noticed the group of college kids starting to leave their chairs. They looked my way and waved goodbye.

"Thanks!" they hollered and smiled, showing their appreciation for the beer.

As I scanned the beach, most other beachgoers were already gone or packing their belongings to leave. There was no one within fifty yards of us. I assumed happy hour had begun at the bars on the other side of the road; however, we preferred to remain on Perissa Beach to enjoy the tranquility.

Chapter 13
Up and Very Down

Two people can feel each other's love. Yet, when they are able to feel the other's pain, they better understand love.

We were standing at the Messa Vouno trailhead. The massive rock rose sharply upward and towered over Perissa. Just below us a group of donkeys and their handlers stood by a weathered, three-sided lean-to, offering rides up and down the mountain. We glanced over and gave a friendly nod, but had little interest in riding the tired working animals. To our surprise, the worn trail started upward on a fairly gradual slope.

Our morning was off to a late start, not because we'd slept in, but because of our relaxed pace. At breakfast, we'd had a chance to visit with some of Diane's friends who had arrived from Athens for her party and a few of the relatives who had arrived at the hotel. Mingling and introducing ourselves to the new faces had felt celebratory and I'd started to look forward to the party, feeling thankful for our flight change.

Diane's friend, Brigitta, had suggested we start our hike in Kamari and trek to the top to view Ancient Thira and then return by the same route. She'd said the road going up from Kamari was paved most of the way and there were benches along the route that offered shady spots to rest and rejuvenate. However, Sara wanted to make sure that she visited the Chapel of Panagia Katefiani, which was the small church embedded in the side of the cliff on the Perissa side. Therefore, we once again took the water taxi to Perissa to begin our hike.

"It doesn't look too bad," said Sara.

"Not now, but it'll get steeper." I was forever the realist.

"You can see other people going up and some coming down, so it isn't impossible."

"We'll take our time. Might as well get started."

When we walked along the store fronts in Perissa, I stopped at a small store and bought some water to add to my beach tote. I knew that we needed to be prepared for this hike. It was less than twenty-four hours from when we were in this same village relaxing and enjoying the beach. Since I was totally relaxed today, I wouldn't have minded hanging out at the same spot across from the Tranquility Bar again.

On the other hand, Sara was bold and didn't want to miss anything, which is why we were heading up from the trailhead—no beach time for us!

We shuffled upward. Sara again assumed the lead with a determined focus to first reach the chapel and then the top of Messa Vouno where Ancient Thira awaited. The grinding sound of shoe soles against the hardened trail defined the pace and the rhythm of our steps. It was a sound that seemed to warn us about the rigorous climb ahead.

There were only a few comments exchanged between us. The noise generated from our steps, mixed with our own heavy breathing, seemed to detract from the effort to speak loud enough for us to hear each other. Yet again, the inspiring scenery spoke boldly to us.

The hiking path zigged and zagged continually upward. It felt inspiring and I was surprised at our progress. After only a few minutes, we were already looking down on Perissa. The flat land that served as a base for the village contrasted sharply with the rugged, rocky terrain in front of us.

Sara paused. "I bet it takes us about half an hour to get to the chapel."

"You may be right, at least to where the path goes across to the chapel."

Pointing toward the village, Sara said, "Do you see the big church in Perissa's square? That's Timiou Starvro. Like everything else in the village, it was destroyed during the 1956 earthquake, so most of the stuff down there along the beach was built in the '60s."

"And how do you know that?"

"I read it on a tourist sign while you were buying the water."

"Well, thanks for being the tour guide."

"We really are getting higher much quicker than I thought."

We were making progress. The entire village of Perissa lay below us and we could see well beyond its boundaries. We could easily view the entire black sand beach and the road that ran along it. The church Sara pointed out seemed to be the focal point of the village. Its vivid blue dome drew our eyes towards it.

"How are you doing, Sara?"

"Not bad. That beach looks beautiful from up here. It's a 'blue flag' beach. That's what they designate as the best beaches."

"Another sign?"

"Yup. You have to be observant."

"Who needs an iPad when I have you?"

"Hey, thanks for doing this. Cross this off our island bucket list."

As I watched Sara hike up the path, I realized that I was more relaxed now than at any time during the week. I was so relieved that Sara knew about the kid's separation. In fact, I was surprised at how well she was handling it. The dilemma of telling or not telling no longer weighed heavily on my shoulders. We were ready to support each other and counsel them in any way needed. It also was a relief to know our travel arrangements home were complete. It was one of those nagging details that needed to be resolved. We were rebooked and this vacation, despite some issues, had truly been wonderful. With all in order, I felt that the remaining days had the potential of being the best of the entire trip.

Sara stopped in front of me, "May I have a drink of water?"

"No problem." I dug the bottle from my tote.

The water was still cool and probably, at the moment, tasted better than the beer on the beach. It was an infusion we both needed. Our climb had quickly taken us above the village and the chapel path was less than 100 yards away. However, I had to admit that the mid-day sun was warmer than I had expected. The sun had risen over the ridge and was now hovering directly above the barren mountain we were climbing. There was very little opportunity to find shade.

The sweat seemed to be seeping from my pores faster than I could put water into my body. I thought we should take an opportunity to rest before we diverted onto the side trail to the chapel. I expected the direct sun had to be affecting Sara.

"Sara, let's sit down and take a break here before we head over to the chapel."

"Okay, but there's no shade anywhere. I'm not sure a break is going to give us much relief. We might toast in the hot sun."

"Yeah, I know. I didn't think it would be so intense. Happy hour in Perissa sounds real inviting about now," I laughed. "If we turn back now, we can have an early cocktail at Tranquility."

"No way, I'm going to the chapel. It's a once-in-a-lifetime experience."

With the path to the chapel right off to our side, we leaned against a large rock to give our weary bodies some support. Though our backs were to the sun, the rays persisted in torching our shoulders. That forced both of us to sit on the ground against the rock in an effort to shield our bodies from the direct sunlight. Glancing at Sara, I could see the shimmer of sweat on her brow. I handed the water bottle to her again.

"We're going to finish this bottle before we get to the top," she said with concern.

I glanced in the tote. "I have another."

"How bad do you think that path to the chapel is?"

"Well, lots of people have walked it before us, but it doesn't have guard rails."

Sara took a deep breath. "I know, but I want to do it. I can't chicken out now."

"If you think you can handle it, we'll do it."

Sara glanced towards the trail. She stood on her tippy toes and peered across the ledge that ran along the cliff. There were a few spots that would certainly challenge Sara's aversion to heights. Taking a deep breath, she said, "I'm going to try. You can go first and I'll keep my eyes on you. I won't look down. Just stay right in front of me."

"I will, but remember yesterday. Be honest with yourself. If you don't want to do it, we can just keep hiking to Kamari."

"I'm honest enough with myself to know this won't be easy, but I need to be persistent enough to do it. It's my one chance."

I nodded and reached to give her a reassuring rub on her shoulder. We stood up and diverted from the main trail to the path that led across the face of the cliff to the chapel. We moved slowly and cautiously. The trail was narrow and the edges of the rock worn. It wound around enormous boulders and across a ledge that was about 300 yards above Perissa. It was only about 50 yards to the chapel, but we'd need to side-step most of the way until we found a wider foundation of rock around the chapel itself. It definitely would challenge Sara and me.

Sara moved stiffly. I could feel her hand grip my shoulder with the pressure increasing each time we crossed a section along the ridge. The side-stepping motion of each carefully placed step created a scraping sound that almost raised the hair on the back of my neck. I knew I needed to remain calm to help ease Sara's anxiety.

I also knew this was not a simple task for Sara, but like many other occasions in life, her determination would serve her well. It also was evident that she didn't want to miss this opportunity. Though she said little and appeared to fix her eyes on my shoulder, she was making steady progress. Occasionally, I saw her glance at her feet, securing one and sliding the other toward it.

Within a few minutes, we inched our way to the small Chapel of Panagia Ketefiani. It looked like any other Greek church only on a smaller scale, being about fifteen feet by twenty feet. It was painted in the traditional blue and white colors. One could easily see why this was a place of refuge, it would be incredibly difficult for intruders to reach this point, especially if the villagers were defending it.

Sara moved to the back corner of the church. She gripped the wooden trim and looked out over Perissa. She seemed to let down her guard and the edges of her lips almost appeared to be smiling.

"Made it!" she exclaimed with obvious satisfaction.

"I'm proud of you, dear! I wasn't sure you could do it."

"I know and to be honest, I wasn't sure I had it in me. There were a couple of spots where my legs didn't want to move."

"You did it. Nice job. This chapel is dedicated to the Virgin Mary, so she may have been watching over you."

"She may have, but this church really is a sanctuary. It may be the safest place on the island," said Sara, now that she was in a secure spot.

"It's a small building, but it symbolizes so much. I bet the people who came here in the late 1500s for refuge must have built a church here really feeling the Virgin Mary would protect them."

"That sounds fitting. Churches throughout history have provided sanctuary."

"But this one physically protects those around it by allowing access via one narrow route."

"The church must have taken some time to build. Bringing the materials up the mountain would have been quite a challenge."

There was a pause as we both scanned the path we'd just climbed. To me there was a sense of accomplishment, but to Sara it appeared to provoke some deeper thought.

"Do you ever feel like this is a dream?"

"It's surreal. Only you and me and this view."

We moved over to a large rock a safe distance from the cliff. It felt secure and gave Sara some additional time to relax. The nearby chapel also helped shade us from the sun. From our cliffside perch, it was easy to see the movement of people on the beach below. If we were ancient Greeks, we'd be able to see anyone approaching the island by water or moving along the beach. It was a spot that seemed to reveal an insight to the early Greeks who sought refuge here.

As I continued scanning the amazing view around Perissa, I couldn't help but be inspired. "I never thought in a million years I'd be here perched on the side of a cliff in Greece."

Sara chuckled, "I know. It's amazing. This island was the perfect escape."

"Perfect," I said, laughing. "I am so glad we reached out and grabbed this piece of life."

"Life is full of great experiences," added a philosophical Sara. "If you're going to live life to the fullest, you can't put off experiencing all that it has to offer."

"You've been quite philosophical on this trip, but I'm not going to disagree. We've always been good about staying out of ruts in our life, but we can do so much more now that we're retired."

"At this stage of my life, I don't want to look at what I can accomplish. I want to focus on what I can experience."

"You really did get an extra cup of Zen on the beach yesterday."

Sara looked amused. "Just appreciating life."

"You should. We've had a great life together."

Sara smiled at my expressive comment. "It's been a great week together, one I'll never forget or regret."

After a hug and a little more water, it was time to move on. "I think we're together on this thought. We'd better get back to our hike. The sun is really getting warm."

We started slowly back along the ledge. Since Sara didn't want to look ahead, she asked me to go first again. With her hand on my shoulder and her eyes fixed on the trail, we moved cautiously toward the main trail. I sensed Sara was now a bit more confident for the return trip. The sun was beating on the solid rock surface. It heated our bodies and the humidity in the air was uncomfortable. Our slow movement and the sweat drenching our clothes made the short return seem a lot longer.

As we reached the main trail that headed upward to the top of Messa Vouno, we embraced, but didn't completely pull our sweaty bodies together. I immediately reached for the water and offered it to Sara. Without a word, she took a long swig from the bottle. I immediately did the same. Our breathing was heavier.

There was no relief from the intense sun. We were on the mountainside with no trees to provide shade. The barren landscape left us vulnerable to the sun's rays.

Sara looked up. "Let's do this. It should take us about thirty more minutes to get to the top and then it's all downhill to Kamari."

"The pool at the Boathouse is going to feel really good, but we have a bit of work to do first."

"Let's get the tough uphill section over with."

On that note, we resumed our climb. Up ahead I could see the switchbacks wind their way to the top. The back and forth path was well-traveled, but steep. On the positive side, there were no more dangerous cliffs. At this point we were on the back side of the mountain and it was more of a steep, grassy, open area. The massive rock blocked much of the breeze from the sea. The temperature seemed to be climbing as fast as we were.

After about fifteen minutes of hiking, Sara stopped in front of me. Her t-shirt was wringing wet and her forehead glistened in the sun. I felt like she looked. I was concerned that the hike was taking a toll on her.

"You need some more water?" She responded by swiping a hand across her sweaty brow. After one deep breath, she opened the water bottle and took a big swig and then immediately wiped her face again.

"You okay?"

"I think so. The heat is getting to me."

"Do you want to rest?"

"No. If I sit down, I'm not sure I'll get back up. Let's get this climb over with."

We again started upward. Our feet thumped the ground, leaving no doubt that our steps were more deliberate and our pace had slowed. The sun beating on our backs only intensified the difficulty of each step. It was probably foolish to start up the mountain mid-day. The daily temperature was at its peak and the sun continued to dog us.

Sara would take about twenty steps and then pause briefly. She would take a deep breath, look up and start again. It was a pattern that seemed to help her cope with the climb. I followed the same pattern since I was behind her. I definitely was feeling the stress of the hike, but knew I had greater endurance than Sara. I was more concerned about her wellbeing.

Sara stopped and turned towards me. "We have one long switchback left."

"Five more minutes. Can you make it?" I asked with concern.

"I think so. Do you have any water left?"

"About half a bottle. It's all yours."

"Thanks. Maybe I could have lived without making it to this part of the island."

"But when you finish, you can say you did it, right?"

"And if I don't, put on my tombstone that I tried."

We continued our trek. I felt a small burst of energy when I saw that the top was within reach. I could only hope the same for Sara. Her slow, methodical steps seemed to indicate otherwise. The back of her shirt was darkened by the sweat from her body. The sweat on her legs heightened the tone of her muscles, but also highlighted the strain of each step. She definitely looked like she'd need a rest before we started our walk down to Kamari. The reality was that the top was only a few steps away, but we had nearly another forty-five minutes of hiking before we'd be at the hotel.

As Sara stepped off the trail onto the parking lot for Ancient Thira, she immediately headed to a bench that overlooked the other side of the mountain. There was a nearby tree that offered minimal, but welcome shade. I sat beside her. I looked at the view of Kamari below and then I glanced back towards Perissa to see the climb we'd accomplished.

"Sara, look back to Perissa. We made quite a climb!"

She glanced back, moving her body as little as possible. "We did it, but I need some time to recover. There's not much *umph* left in me."

"No problem. The path down is paved and there's a lot more shade; plus the sun will be on the other side of the mountain."

"I know," replied Sara, sounding depressed. "Jay, I need down time before we move on."

"Do you want to wander around the Ancient Thira ruins for a while?"

Sara glanced up toward the entrance to the ancient city. There were about fifty steps that led to the ticket window and a path that continued up beyond that to the ruins. She turned her weary face toward me and shook her head 'no.' "You go. I just want to sit here. I really need some time."

"If you're sure."

"Go Jay. I can't do it."

I rubbed her shoulders and kissed the top of her head. I knew from her dejected spirit and the tone of voice that she'd reached her limit. It was best to give her some time to herself. I started up the stairs. My intentions were to take a quick look at the ruins and then return to Sara.

I paid the small admission fee. I was instructed to follow the path to the ancient ruins. Walking on the path which followed the ridge along the top of the mountain, I had an expansive view of Perissa on one side on the mountain and Kamari on the other. Though the views were impressive and the ridge provided a unique perspective of both sides, I was thankful that Sara had decided to take some time to rest. Walking the ridge would have been challenging for her and she really didn't need the additional stress that the narrow path would have provided.

The ridge and the view off both sides made me feel like I was on top of the world. The hike was a lot more strenuous than we had figured, but now being on top brought a great sense of accomplishment. I paused for a moment to enjoy this euphoric feeling. My body felt exhausted, but my mind was calm. I was planning to enjoy these last days to the fullest.

After a short walk, the ruins of Ancient Thira were in front of me. This was once the urban center of Santorini in the 9th century BC. The remnants of stone columns, a trademark of early Greece, still stood in many spots. The foundations of ancient buildings were visible across the mountain top. According to the information I received upon entering the site, the first excavations of these buildings started back in 1895 and then resumed again in 1961. I was immediately impressed by the stone work. You had to wonder how the early builders cut the rocks and brought their materials to this site. Some of the inscriptions on the stonework were the oldest examples of the Greek alphabet.

Though I found it all very interesting, I made a quick swing through the ruins. I wanted to get back to Sara quickly. Returning across the ridge, I was again overwhelmed by the views of both sides of Messa Vouno.

Approaching the parking lot, I could see that Sara had moved to a bench that was more in the shade. Her back was toward me, as she was facing towards the Kamari side. I could see that she was hunched over with her elbows braced on her knees and her hands supporting her face. She appeared to be looking at the ground rather than out over Kamari Beach.

When I was about twenty yards away, I cheerfully yelled out, "Honey! I'm back." She moved slightly, but didn't turn my way. I immediately started to worry if she was okay. I approached from behind just as she was slowly sitting up. I put my hands on her shoulders as she turned towards me. Her eyes were red and tears were dripping down her face. I was alarmed.

"Are you okay? Are you having a heat stroke?"

Sara turned toward me and made a sort of grimacing smile. She wiped her tears with her forearm and sniffled.

"Honey, what is it? You okay?"

She didn't respond. She sniffled more and nodded 'yes.' She almost appeared to be embarrassed that I'd found her crying. She looked away and continued to move her head and clear her eyes. I sensed she was trying to mask her true feelings. Something was definitely wrong.

I gave her a minute to collect herself. Actually it was more like twenty seconds, which felt like an endless amount of time. "What is it, Sara? Are you okay?

Through her tears, she said, "I haven't been honest. I'm keeping something from you..."

Sara immediately started to weep uncontrollably, with her face buried in her hands. I slid onto the bench next to her. I put my arm around her and pulled her closer to me. I didn't know what to think and I was starting to panic.

"What is it? Do you need help?"

She shook her head indicating a negative response. Though I understood the response, I couldn't decipher the real concern or her muttering. She remained in her hunched position. Her sobbing made it difficult for her to talk, let alone breathe.

"Let's just sit here a minute. No matter what it is, we'll work it out."

She muttered, "I should have said something."

I didn't say anything for the next minute. While I waited, I rubbed the back of her shoulder blades, trying to console her. Her tears and sniffles subsided.

She took a few deep breaths. She was now in a more upright position and had removed her hands from her face. I continued to wait, occasionally saying, "It'll be okay." Her breathing started to get deeper and shoulders straightened. I remained by her side in a show of support.

She wiped her forearm across her eye and then repeated the process with her other forearm and eye. I saw that her eyes were bloodshot. Though it was difficult for her to talk, she sputtered, "Jay..."

"What is it?"

"I have cancer."

I gasped and embraced her. "Oh honey," were the only two words that found their way over my lips. Sara resumed crying and tears began to pour from my eyes. We gripped each other tightly and held the embrace.

Half crying and half speaking, I found a way to say two more words, "What type?"

Now almost to the point of hyperventilating, Sara forced out one word: "Bad."

That brought a flood of tears from both of us. Our embrace tightened. I tried to control the flow of tears. "I love you."

Wiping her tears away, Sara looked at me. I could now see her steel blue eyes despite the redness. Gasping for breath, she said, "I love you too."

We eased our embrace and turned so that we were both facing the Kamari side. We were both gasping for air attempting to calm ourselves. I tried to think rationally. I didn't even know what type of cancer. I needed to settle down and listen to any information that Sara could provide. I told myself to be strong for her. There are a lot of successful cancer treatments. I slowly inhaled until my lungs were filled to capacity. Exhaling helped ease the tension. Sara appeared to be doing the same.

"Just relax, Love. When you're ready to talk, let me know. I'm here for you."

She nodded her head affirmatively and kept inhaling deep breaths. The flow of tears was slowing and she was collecting herself enough to talk. I waited, trying to show a calm face, but inside my guts were turning in knots and my heart was racing.

When had this started? Why hadn't I noticed? Why didn't she tell me? Suddenly I started putting the pieces together. She'd been physically tired, her need to re-examine our relationship, the philosophical thoughts, and, of course, the insistence on leaving the ship. I had sensed something was bothering her, but I didn't expect anything like this. The thoughts raced around my head.

Inhaling one last deep breath, Sara turned to face me. I could see the pain in her eyes. She spoke softly. "I had an abnormal mammogram—actually, two of them."

"They both showed the same thing?"

"Yes, both showed a growth."

"Oh, Sara."

"Jay, let me explain," she said, somewhat agitated. "I had a second mammogram about two weeks ago. It confirmed that I have a tumor about two centimeters in size. Just before we left, I went in for an ultrasound and a needle biopsy to check if the cancer was in the lymph nodes under my arm."

"What—"

Stopping me mid-sentence, Sara said, "I don't know all the facts. I have to go in to get the full diagnosis. It isn't good, Jay."

"They've come a long way in treating breast cancer. Maybe..."

"Jay, I need to find out how severe it is and then they will work on a treatment program. I had an appointment for the first day back, but I asked to have it moved later in the week since we're staying an extra night."

It felt like my heart was now in the pit of my stomach. The most important person in the world to me was very ill. I wanted to do all I could to help her.

"We can catch the first flight out tomorrow and get you to your scheduled appointment. The money doesn't matter."

Showing a sincere, but wan smile, Sara responded, "Oh Jay, thanks, but I can wait. I was always looking forward to this vacation, but it became even more important to me after the diagnosis."

"Sara, you're the most important person in my life. You're everything to me. Forget about the vacation. I don't think we should delay our trip home or any treatment they may prescribe."

"I've grappled with this for about three weeks now. I made the decision to come here while I wait for the results. I'm not going to let it rule my life."

"I hear you, Sara, but don't delay things. I want the best for you. We'll get you the best treatment."

"I expect it is going to be a long road...probably radiation and chemo. They may even have to remove part or all of my breast."

"Oh, babe, I'm not sure what to say, but let's think positive."

"I will, but I've already been sad, mad as hell, and scared. Probably still am all three. Life just isn't that Goddamn simple."

As I nodded in agreement, not really knowing what to say. I knew this was going to be a tough road for her. I sensed by her emotions that she already was dealing with the reality of cancer. I knew I felt terrible, but she was the one who was already dealing with it.

There was a brief silence that hung in the air. It pounded at me. It was one of those times where someone should say something, but none of my words could provide the appropriate response. We shared a brief glance before we looked out over the vistas of the village below, yet never really focused on anything. The silence grew louder as I searched for the right words. My mind had eliminated all other things.

Sara finally spoke. "We go home the day after tomorrow. That gives us less than two days to enjoy this remarkable place. I need to soak in all the energy from this beautiful island so I can face reality when I get home."

"We can do that, but we need to keep communicating honestly together."

"I will. I don't want to keep anything from you. I didn't want to ruin your vacation. I just want to appreciate this time. It's all about time."

"Don't say that."

"I know the seriousness of this and have had other friends deal with it. It's going to turn our world upside down whether we like it or not. The next couple of days are our last chance to be carefree. I'm dealing with it and it's not going to fuck up my vacation."

"Okay, I have no issues. I'm here to support you."

"I'm sorry if I sound mad. I'm mad at the cancer—not at you!"

"I know, sweetie."

Sara stood up. "Shall we start our hike down?"

"That hike up was brutal, I can get us a cab at the drop off point for Ancient Thira."

"No way. The hike up was torture, but hiking down there's shade, so the sun won't fry us."

"We can ride, it's only two miles to the hotel. It wouldn't cost much."

"You don't get it! I'm not giving in to this hike or the fucking cancer. We'll hike down."

"Damn, you're determined." I wrapped my arm around her.

"It'll give me a run, but I can be stubborn, as well as determined. Let's kick some ass."

"Then let's do it."

We started down the winding, narrow road that would lead us to Kamari. The road itself was barely wide enough for two small cars to pass each other, yet it was wide enough for us to walk side by side. It was the first time during all our island hikes that we were able to walk side by side for any length of time.

The sun had beat on us coming up from Perissa and I probably would have enjoyed a ride down in a taxi, but there seemed to be a purpose in pushing ourselves to complete the full hike over Messa Vouno. There were lots of questions and thoughts swirling in my mind, but outwardly I walked tall and held onto Sara's hand.

As we made our way along the road descending into Kamari, I pointed to the far end of the beach. "You can see the Boathouse from here...over there where that tree line ends."

Sara glanced in that direction and nodded. After a few more strides, I felt her grip my hand and then she paused. "Look at how the colors from the field blend with the white buildings at the edge of the village. It looks like an angel," she said.

I gazed over to the area near the edge of town and responded affirmatively, "I think I see it."

"Let's take that as a sign," she whispered.

Chapter 14
Morning After

Life will bring hardships. Relationships are tested in these difficult times. Partners can choose to respond in a way that is destructive to the relationship or they can combine their inner strengths to address the challenges together. Strong relationships will endure.

I felt terrible. The morning sunlight streaming through the curtain on the balcony door was more of a blaring alarm than a gentle awakening. The glare forced one eye to close and the other to squint at the barely recognizable surroundings of our room. As I turned my head away from the blinding light, I felt a jarring pain in the side of my head. My stomach swirled, but I couldn't decipher if I needed food or abstinence. Bad news and wine apparently didn't sit well with me.

Our hike down the mountain yesterday had pushed us to our limits. The time on the trail had taken its toll physically, but the strain from Sara sharing her diagnosis left us both dazed. Walking hand in hand most of the way down, Sara had a chance to share the details of her visits to the doctor's office and encounters with medical procedures. It was difficult to hear the specifics, but I listened intently, trying to grasp the severity of the situation.

Upon our return to the Boathouse, we removed the sweaty, sticky clothes from our bodies in exchange for our swimsuits. We immediately headed down to the pool. The plunge in the water brought smiles and a renewed source of energy to both of us. We bobbed playfully in the water, submerging our heads completely to cool our bodies. There were heartfelt embraces and meaningful kisses. It was an oasis that provided relief to our bodies and souls.

At the tables between the pool and the outdoor bar, Diane's family and friends had congregated for a pre-birthday cocktail hour. I sensed their celebratory mood, but it seemed to contrast with our distressed physical and mental state. In fact, I tended to keep my back towards the group as if to shield us from the upbeat atmosphere.

Soon the group motioned to us to join them. I started to politely decline, but Sara shouted, "We'll be right over." My reaction probably indicated my surprise, but I had no time for a rebuttal. Sara moved towards the pool steps. She turned and smiled at me. Needless to say, I was speechless.

"We have only two nights to enjoy. I don't want to waste any time."

"Okay," I muttered. Before I stepped out of the water, she had tied a beach wrap around her waist and was starting to mingle. Her transition from swimwear to evening wear was as quick as her transition from emotionally drained to social butterfly. I smiled, admiring her transition and character.

The social time seemed to be exactly what Sara needed and seeing her enjoy the time was exactly what I needed. We met some wonderful people who had come from many places to celebrate Diane's 50th birthday. There were plenty of introductions, creations of new friendships, and probably far too many pitchers of local Greek white wine. It was a festive, upbeat evening that seemed to push the bad news aside.

In the morning, with the white wine apparently still in my system, I silently slid out of bed. Sara was lying motionless on the bed with the sheet partially draped over her body. Her long, toned legs stretched along the edge of the bed. The haze in my head was hindering my ability to focus, but I could see that her arm had tucked the sheet over her back, exposing one of her breasts. As my eyes cleared, her beautiful, soft, sensual body part came into focus. Only a couple of days ago I marveled at the beauty of her breasts on Red Beach. I recalled the playfulness of the sparkle in her blue eyes as she sat topless waiting for me to return from a dip in the sea. Yet, this object of adornment was threatening the one person I most cared about. I looked at it as the enemy.

My own body was telling me that there was an immediate need for coffee. I thought back to last night, the continuous urging from Spyros to have one more glass of wine brought a smile to my face, along with a sharp, searing pain in my head. Greek hospitality had gotten the best of me or maybe I just needed to escape.

I grabbed my iPad and headed down to breakfast. The beautiful blue sky and sunshine forced me to put on sun glasses. Most of the guests who had congregated at the bar last night were now seated at the breakfast tables. As I surveyed the crowd, they were all in a much more upbeat mood than I was.

I felt a tap on my shoulder; I turned to see a smiling Spyros. He grinned and asked, "Do you need one more glass of wine?"

That brought a chuckle from both of us. "No, but I could use a coffee."

He was holding a cup and saucer. "I have a special Greek coffee for you. It will help get you going today."

"Thanks," I said, gratefully accepting the coffee.

"Gotta get going, we have a birthday party in five hours," he said, grinning.

That brought a few laughs from the surrounding tables. I exchanged greetings with many of my new friends, but declined offers to sit with them. I jokingly said I needed time to recoup alone, but even in my damaged state, I wanted to spend some time on my iPad researching breast cancer. I needed to know more.

After passing through the breakfast buffet, I settled in at the most secluded table. My first bite of the creamy Greek yogurt, drizzled with sweet honey, seemed to sooth my churning stomach. One gulp of the rich, dark coffee helped clear my foggy brain. My demeanor immediately started to improve. I inhaled the moist sea air. It felt good, so I repeated the process and let my muscles relax.

I glanced down at my iPad and typed "breast cancer" in the search bar." I followed the links to an article on the Stages of Breast Cancer. My eyes quickly scanned the charts and text trying get an overview of the disease and its progression.

The stages ranged from zero to four. I started at the bottom, the zero stage indicated that no cancer cells were found, a non-invasive breast cancer. It appeared that Sara was past this stage. Stage one was divided into two areas. My eyes quickly focused on the category 1A that indicated a tumor not more than two centimeters was found, but it had not moved out of the breast. I was sure Sara had said centimeters in describing her tumor but that now seemed so large. Did she say centimeters or millimeters?

My heart was pounding fast, as I quickly scanned the information in Stage two. It also was divided into categories and then sub-categories, so it made it difficult for me to pinpoint anything specific to Sara; however, I did see information that focused on tumors about two centimeters in size. The difference in the categories seemed to focus on whether the cancer had spread to the lymph nodes and I know that was a concern for Sara.

Stage three injected fear into me. The common element in this stage was that the cancer had spread, possibly to the lymph nodes, chest wall, or bones. Without even understanding all the technical sections of this stage, I knew the treatments would be difficult. I realized that if Sara was diagnosed with any form of stage three cancer the battle would be extremely tough.

I hesitated to look at Stage four. How could it be any worse? The description for this stage was short. It detailed that it was an invasive cancer that spread beyond the breasts to the lymph nodes and other organs; such as the lungs, bones, liver, and brain. There wasn't much more to read and I didn't want to read it anyway. What I did read seemed to dampen my hopeful spirit.

I knew I had to take a peek at the treatment options, which were linked to each stage. I started with stage two, feeling that maybe that's where Sara's symptoms would fall. As the chart of treatments popped up on my screen, almost immediately my eyes shut and I took a deep breath. I was preparing myself and hoping for the best. My eyes were drawn to words on the list: mastectomy, radiation, lumpectomy, chemotherapy, hormone therapy, and targeted therapy. I didn't expect such drastic treatments for stage two. I feared for Sara. All kinds of fearful thoughts entered my mind. The reality of cancer was hitting me like a car running into a cement wall. There appeared to be no good options. I wondered if Sara had looked at a chart like this.

I didn't want to, but I forced myself to look at the level three treatments. I only glanced briefly, but the same words flew off the page at me. Though when I looked at 3B, the word "inoperable" forced me to look away and take a deep breath. This could not only be a battle, but a war. I needed to be strong for Sara.

In need of hope, I continued my search by typing in "Breast Cancer Survivors." As I scanned down the list of links, "Breast Cancer Stories," caught my attention. Clicking on the link brought up many testimonials of women who had gone through treatment. It was difficult to read their words, as most had a very painful physical and emotional journey. Trying to keep a positive outlook, I told myself to focus on the fact that they were survivors.

They outlined the turbulent days of waiting for the diagnosis, the emotions, and the fears of the unknown. I thought of Sara and her choice to escape to Santorini. Though I'm sure she feared the worst, she decided to forge ahead in life and follow through with the vacation we had dreamed about. It amazed me that she opted to extend her vacation, leaving the ship to await her full diagnosis. I admired her courage and lust for life, but it worried me.

Each woman on the site—and there were literally hundreds, shared their grueling rounds of treatments; the radiation, chemo, lumpectomies, mastectomies, and array of other options that challenged them to their inner core. All were pushed to their limits and beyond. Their family, work, and personal routines were re-routed on a tumultuous roller coaster of challenges. However, they were survivors.

Though my head was clearing and my stomach improving, my body was tense and my heart was aching. It appeared whatever the prognosis, Sara would face a difficult road ahead of her. I glanced down the road that ran along the beach and the outdoor restaurants. I recalled Sara looking at the older couple and asking me if I'd be there to support her as we aged. Obviously, at the time I didn't understand the urgency of her concern. She'd been searching for a commitment from me. I needed to communicate my total commitment to her and ensure her that I'll be at her side throughout this ordeal. She should not feel as if she's facing cancer by herself.

I glanced up from my tablet to see Sara standing on our balcony. She was wearing her white wraparound beach cover up. The sun was shining brightly on her robe, outlining the soft silhouette of her body under the light gauze material. Her hair fluttered in the breeze. I watched her deeply inhale the sea air. Her chin was raised up and her eyes appeared closed. It was as if she was claiming the moment to relax. Though, if she was like me, she might also have been searching for a way to flush the wine out of her system.

As she lowered her chin, she looked down at me and smiled. Her slight wave seemed to signal to me that she was in good spirits. She blew me a kiss and mouthed, "Be right down." I decided to close down my iPad and wait.

Within a couple of minutes, Sara made her way down the steps. Her hair was pulled back in a ponytail. She was wearing a pair of shorts and a t-shirt. She smiled and walked lightly on her bare feet. The extra hour of sleep seemed to agree with her. She approached the other tables extending morning greetings and sharing stories of last night. I intently watched as she patted shoulders, laughed, and waved at others across the tables.

Grasping a much-needed cup of coffee, she headed to the nearby buffet area. As she spoke to Barbara and Anna, the hotel's housekeepers who were replenishing the Greek yogurt and ham, she seemed relaxed and full of life. When she turned toward me, Spyros playfully asked if she needed another glass of wine.

She replied, "Soon! We have a party in four hours."

Inwardly, I smiled. What an incredible woman!

She had every right to feel down, depressed, upset, and maybe even hung over, yet she'd waltzed down the staircase into the courtyard like a princess entering the ball. She greeted all around her and took a moment to connect with each person. Her bright smile complemented the morning sunshine and there was an aura of happiness around her. I was amazed to see her in such a wonderful mood, but wondered what emotions were hidden behind her smile.

Cheerfully, Sara leaned down and gave me a kiss.

"Good morning, dear. I love you," she said.

"I love you too. I take it you slept well."

"Actually, I did. The last hour just snuggling in bed with the sunshine coming in was heaven."

"Good for you."

"How did you sleep, Jay?"

"Not so good. I tossed and turned. Lots to think about. Too much wine didn't help either."

Sara laughed, "The wine is your own fault and maybe Spyros contributed. I'm sorry if my issues kept you up."

"Your issues are our issues. It's not an issue of keeping me awake, I just want to do the right things."

"I know, sweetie."

"You honestly weren't awake all night?" I asked, sounding skeptical.

"I think it was the best night's sleep I've had on this trip. I was more relaxed. Jay, I was relieved to share the secret with you. I didn't know how you would react. Besides, this is the first day I don't have to face cancer by myself."

"Sara, you know I'm going to be there for you. You shouldn't think twice about that."

"I know that, though the reassurance is nice. It's the reality that's going to be tough."

"We'll get you the best treatment. We have good insurance."

"I know we will," she replied softly, glancing down. "Remember when you asked me if you tell me you love me too often?"

"Yeah, and you said I could never say it too often."

"And I will still respond that way; yet it's the part that worries me most right now."

"Why?"

"Probably a dozen times a day you tell me that you love me and along with that you tell me how beautiful I am."

"I mean it!"

"I know you do, but what about if I'm no longer beautiful? What if I'm scarred or disfigured?"

"Oh Sara, don't even think that."

"But I do. What's at the end of this struggle? If I survive, what's the end result? It scares me."

"You're going to survive. Thirty-five years together means something. We're in this together."

"We are, but there are lots of questions and issues ahead of us." She paused. "I have to shut it off. Sorry, can we change the subject? It's our last full day on the island."

"Sure," I said. "It's now Santorini time, but I do want you to know that when you need to talk, I'm here to listen."

"Okay," she said. She took a deep breath. "You're right, it's Santorini time and we have to buy a birthday gift before the party."

"Oh, good thinking. With everything else, I almost forgot about that."

The rest of breakfast was pleasant. We tried to ignore the pressing issues related to Sara's health. She was right. We needed additional information before we had to make some difficult decisions. Her plan was to enjoy Santorini, so being a plan guy, we stuck with Sara's plan.

Several other hotel guests stopped by our table. The focus of the conversations centered on the party. It appeared Sara wasn't the only bar patron last night who awoke unfazed by the constant flow of wine. The mood around the pool seemed to be picking back up after last night. Guests were friendly, energetic, and ready to partake in the celebration of Diane's birthday.

I had to admit, the festive atmosphere was contagious. Whether my sluggish body was a result of an overdose of wine or worn out by the emotional struggles within me, I seemed to be preparing myself to engage in a celebration. Like Sara, I felt it was time to focus on the last day of our getaway.

Sara started to clear her items from the table. "Let's take a walk down along the shops. We'll pick up something for Diane."

"Sounds good. Any ideas what to look for?"

"Not really. We'll browse until we find something," she replied, sounding relaxed.

We strolled down the narrow road that ran between the beachside cabanas and the shops. It was about a week ago that we'd first wandered down this same area looking for a hotel. The Boathouse was a great choice. It was a family owned hotel on the end of the beach. The owners were so welcoming. We met so many new friends and now we were invited to be part of a family celebration.

Since we'd walked down this road many times during the last eight days, we were familiar with many of the restaurant owners who greeted us daily, hoping that we would stop and enjoy a meal with them. Though we declined their current invitations, we stopped briefly to exchange greetings and let them know that we were leaving in the morning. They all wished us well and thanked us for visiting Santorini.

"I'm going to miss this place, Sara. We made the right choice in coming to Kamari."

After taking a deep breath, Sara replied. "To me, this is going to be my 'Safe Place.' I imagine there will be many times that in my mind I'll be sitting on a cabana under the warm sun, sipping a glass of wine, and looking out toward the sea."

"Remember that I'm there with you."

Sara gripped my hand as we half-heartedly nodded *"Kalimera"* to a few shop owners.

"That helps. You know, I planned all along to leave the ship. It was a real escape for me. The conversations about our relationship just happened. It was a nice addition."

"It's always been you and me. You're the most important person in my life. We've always made each other a priority."

"Always good. Let's sit down for a while on that bench and take in the view. I'm getting that feeling that vacation time is running out."

"Okay, but there's still nearly a full day left. We'll have to leave for the airport about 10:00 a.m. tomorrow. Our flight is at noon. Spyros is going to give us a ride."

As we sat on the bench with the view across the black sand, our eyes scanned the beach and out over the horizon. It was a chance to soak in the beauty of Kamari Beach.

With a peaceful look on her face Sara said, "I could sit here for hours."

"Because you like the view or just to relax?"

"That and probably a lot more."

Smiling, I added, "If I bought you a bottle of wine, it would probably be perfect."

Sara smiled softly. "I wouldn't need much more in life—a simple setting, you, and a bottle of wine. Maybe that's the perfect way to spend an afternoon. Let all cares blow away in the breeze."

"It would be, but I believe we have a birthday party to attend first.

Sara took a very deep breath and exhaled, "Then I will just soak in this moment. This escape has exceeded my expectations."

With some hesitation, I replied, "Despite all that interfered with our time, it was wonderful!"

"What interference?"

"Sara, I can't put on a blindfold. I learned my wife has cancer and shared that my son's marriage is on the brink. I have to be honest with myself if I am going to deal with it."

Sara leaned on my shoulder and I put my arms around her. She glanced up at me; her eyes were misty. I pulled her closer to me. Momentarily, we sat in silence. The sea glistened and the breeze soothed our faces. People wandered along the road behind us, vacationing and enjoying the day.

Sara sat up a bit and turned toward me. "I wouldn't trade this week for anything else. I've thought many times about meeting with my doctor, but I couldn't dwell on it. Santorini pulled my mind away. I know I need to be honest with myself when I return home."

"It's okay. You were right about jumping ship. We not only had fun, but we grew a lot on this trip."

Sara giggled through a sniffle and gave me a rueful smile. I rubbed her shoulder. Though there were plenty of people around us, we seemed to be isolated in our own world.

I had to ask. "When are you going to tell the kids?"

"Not 'til we know what the treatment plan is. They have their own worries."

"Okay, not sure what we can do for them."

"Listen and be there for them. We're the parents...that's what we do."

"You're the best listener, Mom. I don't think either one of them wants to disappoint you."

"It's not about me. They'll have to do what's best for them. It may be tough for them and us."

"We all have some rough times ahead."

"We can only deal with it; we can't control it."

"We can at least have a plan to deal with it."

Sara laughed as if to dismiss my comment. "Jay, not now. Life's not that simple. We'll do the best we can, but it's our last day here."

Though I felt strongly about creating a supportive plan, I dismissed the thought of saying anything more. It was our last day and we needed to enjoy this peaceful time while we could. A bit unnerved, I sat gazing at the sea. Sara took more deep breaths, as if pulling every last drop of energy from the island atmosphere.

The eight days on the island allowed us to visit many corners of Santorini that we would've never enjoyed during our short cruise stop. Each day we experienced the beauty and the culture of Greece; yet, we both wrestled with emotional and physical issues. I couldn't imagine how Sara had dealt with her diagnosis by herself for the last few weeks. How did she set her issues aside for this trip? I'd tortured myself over keeping my son's secret from her, but that was nothing compared to the magnitude of her issues. Even now, there was fear developing in me about returning home.

I'm sure the reality of the return trip also weighed heavily on Sara.

Sara stood and pointed across the walkway. "Let's walk to that shop over there. We don't have a lot of time to get a gift."

"Onward then."

We wandered into the shop that had an array of clothing items and artwork. The shop owner greeted us and happily offered assistance. Apparently Sara had some ideas about a gift because she immediately started looking through a stack of shawls.

"I think a shawl for Diane would be a great gift."

"If you think she would like it."

"I do. She sits out with the guests at night and the evening air can be cool. I think she could wrap it around her shoulders and be more comfortable."

"Sounds good to me," I replied, since I didn't have any better suggestions and shopping wasn't an especially favorable experience for me.

After a few questions for the owner, Sara decided on a shawl that sported various shades of blue. It was colorful and would go with the Greek Blue accents of the buildings. Sara was pleased with her selection and the owner provided a colorful gift sack.

"We'd better get back and get ready for the party. I have to do something with my hair."

"And I'd better get my body in gear so I can enjoy a little more wine."

"And also some great food from what I hear," added Sara.

~~~

As we headed back to ready ourselves for the party, my mind wandered to the survivor web site I'd viewed earlier in the day. Many of the women pictured in the testimonials were bald—completely bald. That thought punched me in the gut, causing a sickening feeling throughout my body. It wasn't that the thought of Sara going bald disturbed me as much as the thought of her body being put through the treatments. The testimonials all shared how the radiation and chemo made them ill. It was a fearful experience for anyone and now the one I loved was facing the reality of cancer treatments.

My negative thoughts were interrupted by Sara saying, "I'm going to wear a dress. Do you have something clean that's nice enough to wear?"

Her question pulled me back into the present and made me chuckle. We'd been on this trip for over two weeks and had only done wash in the hotel sink once. My clothing options were limited by the cleanliness of the available items.

"I do have a button up shirt and a decent pair of shorts. I'll probably have to wear the same thing on the plane tomorrow."

"No problem. I'm sure everyone is planning to dress up a bit."

Sara's thoughts appeared to be focused on the party, though additional thoughts about her illness probably wormed their way into her mind. I admired her for grasping every opportunity to enjoy this trip. The party was only an hour away.

As we neared the hotel, I reached for Sara's hand and gave it a slight tug, indicating she should stop. I moved her hand to the side so that she'd turn back toward me. I looked at her intently.

"Have I told you I love you today?"

She smiled. Only about five times—a bit below average."

I grinned and embraced her, giving her a passionate kiss. We held the kiss and as we released, I looked directly into her eyes and said, "I love you...and I always will."

She stared back at me and I could see the fear. Her voice cracked when she asked, "No matter what?"

"No matter what."

Chapter 15
The Celebration

Learn to live in the moment to better appreciate the gift of life. Couples need to cherish each moment they have together. We cannot take our relationship, or life itself, for granted. Live in the moment and love your partner.

I stood on the balcony of our room. Level with the tree tops, I watched people stroll down the walkway. Many glanced at menus in front of the restaurants; no one seemed in a hurry. Most couples seemed to hold hands, occasionally stopping to take a picture. Others glanced up in my direction and simply nodded with a relaxed smile. People moved along looking like they had no cares in the world. This seemed to be a trademark of Kamari. It was almost as if people were intentionally walking slower than their bodies normally moved.

It was a beautiful day full of sunshine. Below in the courtyard, Diane's guests were starting to congregate. Like Sara predicted, most were dressed for the party: casual but nice. Evie and Kelly, the boathouse bartending duo, were handing out a few glasses of wine to those who wanted to get an early start on the festivities. I expected everyone to walk over to the Almira restaurant a few doors down for the birthday celebration soon. It was nearing the top of the hour.

I glanced down at my own attire in an effort to evaluate my clothing. My khaki shorts were clean but traveled. My white, button-up shirt had been washed and dried in the sun. It sported a few wrinkles, but I was comfortable with it. Besides, my clothes seemed to be the least of my concerns.

Sara was putting the finishing touches on her hair in the bathroom. I could see her reflection in the mirror. She held a curling iron in one hand and supported her arm with the other. She displayed a look of casual elegance in her long cotton dress covered with bright, artsy, blue stripes. The dress flowed gracefully around her curvy body. She was beautiful.

It was our last night in Kamari. Glancing out over the beach I had an array of emotions. I recalled the day we rented the loungers and, together, spent the day under the sun doing nothing. That was a memory that created a warm smile across my face. I fondly viewed the restaurants that lined the beach, remembering how we had wandered down a side street to enjoy a delightful meal at the Meli and Thymari restaurant. Kamari had provided us with so many romantic meals. Good food and candle light became a nightly tradition. Turning to my right, Messa Vouno towered over the far end of the beach. The initial feeling of accomplishment when thinking about our hike over the top spiraled downward, erasing the smile from my face. I realized that the mountain would forever be etched in my mind as the place where Sara told me she had cancer. In fact, the week in Santorini--so filled with adventure and quality time with Sara--would also be a place where I confronted some of the most difficult issues in my life.

Movement of people shuffling near the bar rerouted my attention. Most of the guests were now collecting their belongings and moving towards the restaurant. I could see Spyros a short distance up the road checking to see if everything was set at the restaurant. I turned to provide an update to Sara, "The group is heading to the restaurant."

"A bit of lipstick, and I'll be ready."

I stayed planted on the balcony, gazing out over the edge. I was ready to leave and had been for the last 20 minutes, but I didn't want to rush Sara. If there is one lesson I had learned over the years with her--she was moving as fast as she could, so I shouldn't try to rush her.

"Ready," Sara cheerfully exclaimed standing in the middle of the room.

I turned around, "You look wonderful. Very pretty!"

"Ahhh, I knew there was a reason I keep you around. Thanks!"

"And looking at you in that dress, I think I know why I keep you around."

"Time to go! It's our last night," replied a smiling Sara who reached for my hand.

Like the tourists I had been watching from the balcony, we strolled leisurely over to the Almira. Though we had issues to deal with, the peaceful walkway of Kamari and the anticipation of the birthday party generated a care free feeling for us. I wanted that feeling to continue and intended to make our last night special.

Most of the other guests were seated in the restaurant's outdoor cabana when we arrived. There were two large tables set for twelve with white tablecloths and napkins. It was a beautiful outdoor setting overlooking the beach. Diane was already seated at one table. Her in-laws were across from her, and Spyros and Evie next to her. Though there were a few seats open at their table, we thought we should leave those seats for any other relatives or close friends. We decided to sit at the other table next to a retired English couple, who now made their home in Greece. We had chatted with them the evening before at the hotel bar and enjoyed their company.

Almost immediately, the waiters were placing fava dip, bread, olive oil, and olives on the tables. This was a ritual I was definitely going to miss come tomorrow. Then before I could even think about grabbing a piece of bread, another waiter swung by placing two pitchers of wine on our table. It was as if it were a signal for the party to begin, and the others milling around the tables quickly found a seat.

Introductions were exchanged. Besides the English couple, our table included a couple from Canada, two women from the island who had known Diane for years, and two couples that were longtime friends visiting from Athens. Most we had met earlier in the week, but the two local women were new acquaintances for most everyone, as they were not staying at the hotel.

It only took a moment before someone suggested we start enjoying the wine. The Englishman and one of the guys from Athens did the honors of pouring. As they completed their chore, Spyros stood up at the next table. He welcomed everyone to the party and thanked all for being part of their extended family. It was kind of a strange feeling for us because we had only known the family for one week, yet there was a connection and a welcoming feeling that we certainly embraced. He held his glass high and toasted, "*Yamas!*" A chorus of "*Yamas*" followed and all took a sip of wine in unison.

Diane then stood with a large smile on her face. Immediately everyone gave her a round of applause. Her blushing cheeks showed her apprcciation as she nodded. She then addressed those gathered, "Thank you for all being here. Old and new friends, you are all appreciated and you all make this a special day for me. Though I am the one turning 50, we are all here to enjoy." A round of laughter and applause followed.

I glanced at the pretty girl next to me, which of course was Sara. She had a glass of wine in one hand, a small plate of fava in front of her, and was talking very expressively to the woman next to her. I could hear her laughing as she shared the story of us jumping ship. I smiled within, took a sip of wine and was so glad she insisted that we explore this wonderful island.

I never was one to dwell on the negatives in life but this week was challenging. Yet watching Sara seemed to focus me on the wonderful time we had together; no schedules to follow, lots of time to connect, the insightful conversations, and the opportunity to explore the island. We had made new friends and now became part of an extended Greek family. It may be a turbulent time in our life but a special time also.

I was pulled out of thought by a platter of tomato fritters being placed in front of me. My eyes marveled at the fried, golden nuggets and their wonderful aroma filled the air. That also caught Sara's attention. She loved most anything with tomato and these were hard to resist. I immediately picked up the platter and allowed Sara to be the first to select. We then passed the appetizer platter around the table where the fritters quickly disappeared.

At that point, Diane appeared at our table. She again thanked us for joining her. We expressed our appreciation and wished her a happy birthday. She explained to us that Name Days are usually bigger than birthday celebrations in Greece. Since most Greeks are named after saints, these days are marked by the saint's day of your name. On your Name Day, you would have a party similar to what we are having today. However, she joked that turning 50 was a good excuse for a party in any culture.

Sara, trying to put a positive twist on the benchmark age, said, "Diane, I think the 50's are the best decade. Your kids are old enough to be on their own. You have more time to do the things you want, more time together with your husband, and you tend to travel more. Enjoy it."

Diane appreciated the comments but jokingly replied, "Thanks Sara, I'll think about that as I count the extra wrinkles each year." The table all laughed, but I know Sara really did feel that the 50's were the best decade. They certainly were good to us.

The changes in life after 50 actually strengthened our relationship. The additional time on our hands seemed to slow us down. We had more time to focus on each other and our relationship. Yet, we took time to indulge in our individual hobbies. Sara painted more and volunteered at the art gallery. I enjoyed wandering over to the golf course during the week. I also found some time to do home improvement projects that I had put off for years. Of course, planning for retirement excited us both. This trip being a result of that planning had been something we had anticipated for some time.

The next course arrived, and of course, no meal in Greece would commence without a Greek salad. A huge bowl of freshly cut cucumbers, tomatoes, olives, and capers arrived. The mixture was sprinkled with basil and garnished with large slices of feta cheese. My body, which recently had been on a steady diet of wine, craved the healthy goodness within the salad. The Feta cheese may not rate high on any healthy scale but it complimented the salad well.

Sara eyed the salad and took a generous portion. I think her body needed replenishing as it had been an emotional week for her. She passed me the salad just as the empty pitchers were replaced with new portions of wine. Sara smiled and chirped, "I think the smiles are getting larger and the laughter louder with each serving of wine."

I laughed with her and nodded my head in agreement. We both were enjoying the party and were certainly contributing to the noise level. It was so interesting listening to other people's travel stories. These guests were avid travelers and had been to so many places. Their descriptions and exuberance instilled a sense of wanderlust in me. Though I caught myself realizing that we probably wouldn't be traveling for some time. Our concern was Sara's cancer, and that would take priority in our life.

Amongst the stories Sara turned to me and said, "I want to go to Spain. This end of the table raves about the food, and they say the architecture and art are wonderful."

Being caught off guard a bit, I smiled and responded, "Whatever you want. I would love to travel there." The far end of the table raised their voices and encouraged me to take her. I put up both my hands and indicated no problem from my end. I playfully added, "She always gets what she wants." Sara responded to that with a playful punch on my arm.

Though I would love to go to Spain with my wife, my mind wondered when we would have the chance to go. The dark thoughts stopped me from engaging further with the other end of the table. But I watched Sara interact with genuine and enthusiastic inquiries. The travel bug had nipped her, and it had lifted her spirits. I marveled at how she was projecting herself into future plans.

My end of the table was sharing information about the island. After our active week here, I was able to contribute to the conversations. The Canadian couple was especially interested in the chapel on the side of Messa Vouno. I had no problem providing a detailed description of the trail and the ledge over to the chapel. My descriptions seemed to add to their excitement about the hike, though I did warn them to start early in the morning and avoid the afternoon sun.

Soon the main course arrived: Moussaka, the traditional favorite. The waiter placed a pre-cut piece in front of each of us. The huge portion was large enough that Sara and I could have shared. However this was a celebration, and besides, I thought the extra starches might help to soak up the wine.

As Sara looked up from the steaming plate, she laughed. "Oh boy. Here they come again."

Those around her looked in the direction she had referenced.

"More Wine!" stated one of guests on Sara's end. Sure enough, another round of wine was on the way. No one at the table seemed to decline. It was a very festive group.

Sara glanced my way, "Are you ready for more?"

"If you would have asked me a couple of hours ago, I would have said no, but I'm apparently back in the swing of things."

Singing in tune she responded with, "Kick it in, second wind, you got two more hours to go."

Laughing at her skill for knowing the words to appropriate songs and her use of Jimmy Buffett, I responded, "I've shifted gears, and something tells me there may be more than two more hours to go."

A few people next to me agreed with the possibility of the party stretching into the evening hours. They felt the group already had established good credentials last night for partying. Judging by my headache and swirling stomach this morning, I did not doubt the groups' abilities to extend a party.

The food was delicious; no one seemed to have difficulty in finishing the large portions. Even Sara was scraping the last morsels from her plate. Stuffed and relaxed, people tended to move their chairs back a few inches and find a more relaxed position. The plates were cleared and people continued their conversations. It was amazing to me how easily it was to interact with these people we had only known a week or less.

One waiter brought a plate of baklava to the table for desert. The layers of nuts and honey between thin layers of pastry were too good to resist. Even though we were in no need of additional food or calories, neither of us could pass on this traditional delight. Most others at the table followed our lead.

Another waiter arrived carrying a tray of shot glasses. Without even asking, I knew that the small glasses contained Raki, the traditional after dinner drink made from the left over grape mash. This white lightning was a bit like moonshine in that it had a powerful taste that could kick your ass.

As the last glass was passed out, Spyros again stood. His smile broader and his mood more festive than the first time he proposed a toast. "Friends, I hope you all enjoyed the meal." A round of applause gave him the feedback he was looking for. He nodded his appreciation for the applause and continued, "Let me toast the beautiful day and my beautiful wife. May she enjoy the upcoming year and may we continue to cherish our friendships."

"*Yamas!*" shouted both tables, and like a well-choreographed play, up went all the shot glasses, down went the *Raki*. The amazing meal had ended.

As people plopped their glass on the table, and as if it were on cue, music started across the walkway. Three musicians had set up to play in the courtyard of the restaurant. Our group in the cabana had been so involved in our food, wine and conversations; we didn't even notice them set up.

The beat was festive and fast. People clapped their hands and kept beat with their feet. It was a repetitive, sharp metallic sound that had you swaying with your shoulders. Spyros came to our table, proud of his heritage, he shared, "Traditional folk dance: *Nisiotika*. It means 'island dance,' but on Santorini we call our version *Balos*. It always part of our celebrations. You must dance."

Immediately a group of four women ran to the dance area. They quickly turned to recruit some additional dancers, including some men. Sara didn't need any additional encouragement; she bolted to join them on their first gesture. Within seconds the group had expanded to about ten. Others sitting in the restaurant or passing on the walkway jumped in with no hesitation. All were eager to participate.

The dancers paired off with the music, turning to the right and then to the left. Their movement was a quick, rhythmic, circling motion. Their feet moved quickly with the music, continuously turning their bodies to the right, then the left, and spinning. It was festive and upbeat.

Spyros sat down next to me. I was watching with amusement as Sara picked up on the dance steps.

"She is enjoying. She dances well," said Spyros pointing to Sara.

"She loves stuff like this. Thanks for inviting us. We appreciate it so much."

"You have been great guests. Our relatives and friends have enjoyed meeting you."

"This has been a great week. So lucky to find the Boathouse."

"Too bad I have to take you to the airport tomorrow."

"At least we had a chance to celebrate Diane's birthday but tomorrow morning it's back to reality."

"Look at her enjoy the wavy motion. When they go around the circle it's like the waves rolling up and down. Symbolic."

"I see. What type of instruments are the ones that look like a rounded guitar?"

"Those are *bouzouki*. One of them has three pairs of strings and the other has four pairs."

"They sound like a mandolin," I responded.

"Maybe same type of sound but we have our own type of playing. Greek music you recognize easy. The *bouzouki* is made from one solid block of wood. It has a lower sound."

"You never cease to amaze me. Thanks for the info. Never would have learned all that on the cruise ship."

He slapped my shoulder getting up, "Probably no *raki* on the big boat either."

We laughed as he departed to speak to other guests. Today was a unique opportunity to enjoy the culture of Greece. All week Spyros had shared information and history about the island. He was a pleasant and knowledgeable host.

Without notice Sara grabbed my arm. "You have to join in this dance. We need guys."

I groaned, "Do I have to?"

"Yes!"

To please her, I let her drag me onto the dance floor. Dance was not my favorite past time, nor did I consider it a talent of mine. It was normally something I did to please Sara, though I always enjoyed being with her and over the years had learned a few steps. However, traditional Greek dancing was not in my repertoire.

Diane was waiting in the center of the dance area to give some brief instructions before the music resumed.

She began, "This is a Greek line dance. We are going to stand shoulder to shoulder. Simple steps, one and two, one and two, back, front, one and two, back and front--just go with the flow of the music, ready?"

I laughed. Although she had demonstrated effectively for most, I was a slow learner when it came to dance. The whole time she was counting steps, I was trying to define the steps more logically. In my mind I was thinking, "One step right, one step left, back, forward, right." It was this logical sequence that probably contributed to me looking more like a robot than a traditional Greek dancer.

However, I linked arms and tried the best I could to follow the group. As I stumbled through the chorus line, I caught Spyros having a bit of a laugh at my expense. He motioned with a shot glass in the air, as if to say I needed another glass of *Raki* for rhythm. I could only signal with my eyes and nod my head that I thought he was right.

Sara on the other hand was right in step and appeared as if she had done the dance all her life. Her musical talents well exceeded mine. The smile on her face and laughter between her and the other guests showed that she was truly enjoying this celebration.

I finished the line dance and received a hug from Sara for making an attempt at the Greek dance. I accepted her thanks, and with blushed cheeks, headed back to the table. I wasn't looking for *Raki* but a sip of water and sitting in a chair would do me just fine.

Before I could sit down, Sara grasped my hand. "Walk with me down by the sea. I need a break and a little connecting time."

I smiled and nodded, waiting to speak until we were further away from the music. Being right on the beach, we walked about 50 yards to where the black pebbles crested from the surf. We started to sit down but realized we should grab a lounge chair and sit on that rather than the black sand. I turned one sideways and we sat facing the sea.

Sara appeared so relaxed. She took a deep breath and said, "I am going to miss that sound, listen."

"Oh, me too," knowing what she was referring to.

We both were silent. The waves washed up on to the beach near our feet. You could see the rounded black pebbles roll in the surf. There was a clinking sound as they bumped each other. As the waves pulled back, the pebbles rolled back into the water, you could hear them as they tumbled back into the sea. It was a unique sound that we both will always associate with Kamari Beach.

After a few waves had rolled in, Sara resumed the conversation, "That is such a relaxing sound. I could listen to it for hours."

"It's mesmerizing; you just get caught up in it."

"It really has a therapeutic sound," added Sara

It was a nice break away from the party. The rumbling sound of the pebbles being washed ashore created a barrier between us and everything else. It was another one of those connecting moments.

"I checked my email today. I didn't get anything from the kids," said Sara.

"Probably won't. They want you to enjoy your vacation. Besides we'll be home in another day."

"I know. I guess my thoughts were drifting back home."

"Tommy should still be at the house when we get there. I am sure he will fill us in."

"You know being in your 20's is tough. Trying to figure out what you want to do with your life, job, relationships, money issues. I really do think the 50's are a lot better."

I chuckled a bit, "You honestly wouldn't want to go back to your 20's? Be young again."

"Nope. And FYI, I don't think I'm old now."

I hugged her from the side and only snickered, "We don't seem old do we. At least we don't admit it."

Sara smiled, "You know, I do feel like our time here is ending. Today this celebration is great. But tomorrow will be a downer."

"It will but it's time we get back. You know we can't wait any longer."

"I know, I really know. There is a feeling inside me that tells me so."

"We can't get too down now. We have a party to return to."

"Okay. Just give me a minute to revamp."

I was silent and let the relaxing sound of the waves resume. I glanced at Sara. Her eyes were closed, her breathing deep and slow. I waited quietly.

After a couple of minutes she turned to me and said, "We are always going to remember this trip."

"What will you remember?"

"Everything!"

"Got to do better than that! Where was your favorite glass of wine?" I asked.

"That's almost impossible. Give me a better question."

"Just think about it. You have to give an answer."

Sara pondered for a moment, "If I have to pick one, I'd say the first one. The first restaurant after we came up the cable car."

"Really? Why that one?"

"Because when I took that first sip I said to myself, I did it. I really did it."

"You mean you planned to jump ship and you did it?"

Sara's eyes had a determined look in them. She looked directly at me. "Yes, but it was more than that. It was weird. I was afraid, afraid to stay on the ship and afraid to get off of it."

Concerned I asked, "What do you mean afraid?"

"It was complex. I was afraid to stay on the ship and go home to meet with the doctors. I was afraid to get off the ship because it would delay seeing the doctors. And I was afraid that if I didn't insist on staying on the island I may never have this chance again. Afraid that I would miss this special part of life!"

My eyes were swelling, my emotions swirling and the end of my lips were curling downward. I sniffled and asked, "Did you make the right decision to leave the ship?"

With a stiff smile she nodded and said firmly, "Without a doubt."

With a few tears finding their way out of my eyes I asked, "Still afraid?"

Sara's lips curled and a flow of tears streamed down her cheeks. She gasped for air and leaned into me. I firmly held her, feeling every convulsion her body made. The relaxing sound of the waves had vanished and our world seemed to cave in around us. It was only the two of us, gripping to each other as one. Her body continued to jerk as she struggled for air. I could feel her tears streaming down my arm. I could feel my tears collecting on the back of her hair. The celebration had ceased.

We continued to hold each other for some time. Once Sara was able to breathe and settle her body a bit, she sat up. Wiping her tears away, she took deep breaths to regain her composure. Sniffling and moving her hands across her eyes and cheeks, she said, "That's been building up for a while."

"No need to explain, Sweetie. I can't imagine."

"Thanks for being here. I've cried alone before and there wasn't anyone to hold me."

"I would have been there. Why didn't you tell me?"

Sara looked at me with a slight smile creasing the edges of her lips, "Because you love me too much."

"Love you too much, what does...."

"You would have given up this vacation to be with me. We would've been sitting next to each other in the doctor's office. We worked our whole life to be here. I wasn't going to let this disease take that away from you or me. I would have lost the first battle."

Taken back by her explanation I replied, "But the vacation is not important. You're the most important thing in my life."

"Exactly. That's why we are here together. I wanted to enjoy this now, with you. I wanted to leave the ship because I didn't know when we would have the chance again," staring directly into my eyes she added, "This is part of the journey."

The intent look in her eyes and the inflection in her voice left no doubt that she had thought this through. I knew I had to accept and support her decision. I reached for her hand and gave her a reassuring grip. I took a deep breath and felt the tears starting to escape from my eyes, "I am with you for the entire journey. We'll do whatever it takes to take care of you."

I felt the comforting pressure of her hand in return. She didn't respond but took a deep breath and looked out over the rolling waves. We sat silently. The pebbles rolled up from the sea and back down. We both apparently had plenty to think about.

After a couple minutes, Sara started to collect herself. She stood and fluffed her hair with her hands and brushed the front of her dress. "We should get back soon. I bet I look a mess."

"You look beautiful. Let's take five more minutes to listen to the waves. Then we should be ready to go back."

I, too, needed time to let the redness in my eyes retreat. A few more minutes to recover would do us both good. Rejoining a birthday party after our emotional exchange wasn't the easiest of tasks, but we didn't want to be rude to our hosts.

We stretched our legs out and took deep breathes to relax. I occasionally rubbed Sara's leg or shoulder for reassurance. We didn't say much. It was time dedicated to rejuvenating our spirits and bodies. The soothing sounds of the waves and rolling pebbles were exactly what we needed.

A short time later Sara asked, "How do I look?"

"Like a beautiful Greek goddess," I said as I pushed an out of place section of her hair back in place.

"How are my eyes?"

"Good. You really do look good."

"All right. We should get back."

I held her hand as we started back across the beach. The further we got from the sea, the louder the music became. Judging by the festive noise in the air, the party was in high gear.

We slipped in the side of the cabana and grabbed a glass of wine. The vintage felt good on my throat. Sara smiled as she set down her glass after her first sip. It probably helped to settle her nerves.

Diane was passing the area where we were standing and motioned to Sara to join her on the dance floor. Sara glanced at me, and I encouraged her to go. As Sara trotted out to dance, I could see the color returning to her face and the sparkle coming back to her eyes. She appeared to be happy to return to the dance floor.

The trio played for another 30 minutes. Sara danced several more dances. She definitely burned off the calories from the elaborate meal and appeared to be enjoying the festivities. I learned that I could avoid being called to the dance floor if I was engaged in a conversation. So I had a chance to talk to quite a few other guests and learn more about them and their travels.

As the music ended, all the dinner attendees settled back in around the tables. It was a sporadic seating arrangement, as the two tables kind of merged into a circular formation. People pulled chairs into the area between the two tables, and others sat around the edges. It gave everyone a chance to be part of the conversation.

A few people shared stories about Diane and adventures they had in the past. A couple of them worked with her as a bartender in the early days. Some shared how they met Diane and others chimed in with stories of her meeting Spyros. It was light banter and laughter. The wine consumption had slowed and people were in a relaxed mood.

Theresa, the woman from Canada, sat listening to all the stories. At one point she exclaimed, "This is the most beautiful setting for a celebration and what an amazing day!" Others agreed. They injected descriptions of the glistening sea, the dancing, the music, the soft breeze, the puffy clouds in the sky, and the wonderful food. It truly had been a wonderful celebration. We all thanked our hosts.

Sara, who seemed enthralled by the conversations, turned and said to me, "What have we done in life to deserve to be sitting here?"

There was a bit of silence. I didn't know exactly how to reply.

Sara then added, "We are sitting along the Aegean Sea, in Greece, on a beautiful day, celebrating a birthday of a wonderful new friend. I could never have imagined this. What did we do to deserve this?"

I wasn't sure why she was asking, but I knew she was right about never imagining a day like this. It didn't seem possible. We had not planned this part of our trip in advance and certainly could not have predicted being at this celebration. I could only respond by saying, "Not sure we ever deserve anything in life, but we should always enjoy what it offers at the moment."

Sara smiled and said, "the moment." She paused and added. "Life is about living in the moment."

Chapter 16
Goodbye

We cross paths with many people in life and saying goodbye can be difficult. It's a term that finalizes a relationship or an event. It signals the end to time that we shared. There are times we say goodbye, knowing we will never meet again. There are times we simply don't want to say goodbye.

At 7:30 am, I found myself sitting on the same sun lounger on the beach I had pulled sideways the night before. I'd gotten a good night's sleep because the party had ended in the early evening hours. There were a few guests who spent some additional time around the pool and bar in the courtyard, but Sara and I called it a night knowing that we had to depart in the morning. As usual, I was the first one up and arrived a few minutes early for breakfast. The hotel crew was probably running a few minutes behind due their participation in last night's celebration.

I'd wandered to the beach with a purpose. Sitting on the lounger, I opened my iPad. I tapped on my camera and switched it to video. Leaning it up against the leg of the chair, I framed a section of the beach where the small pebbles washed ashore in the waves. I hit the record button and sat quietly for exactly five minutes. I patiently waited, listening to the pebbles being pushed up the beach and being pulled back down to the sea. The rolling, clinking pebbles played their tranquil tune.

Sara's voice softly whispered in my thoughts, "I could listen to this for hours." That's precisely what she said last night sitting by my side on this very chair. She loved the sound of these waves. They seemed to calm her and put her in a meditative state. I thought by recording the waves and the sounds of Kamari Beach that she could return here during difficult times ahead.

All the talk of travel last night inspired both of us to think of future trips, but this morning making the video intensified my fears of never returning here or never being able to take Sara to Spain. The future seemed uncertain and bleak. Our life of so many years together had some challenges, but had been filled with simple pleasures and quality time. Now things weren't so simple and time was a term I wanted to avoid.

Tommy and Kathy's separation was a concern. As a parent, it's heart-wrenching to watch your child go through a difficult time, but you understand it's life—it's a process they have to go through to better understand life for themselves. You offer support and make sure they understand that you're available for them when needed. I was prepared to support my son and was set to return home.

Clutching my iPad and staring at the footage I just captured, I knew someday Sara would appreciate it. Maybe I'd save it for when she was having a difficult day. I was hoping it could be something that would lift her spirits, a bit of a surprise, an opportunity to return here and bring back happy memories. I dreaded and was frightened by the thought of seeing her go through cancer treatment. I could almost recite verbatim the testimonials from the breast cancer website. I knew it would be a difficult road for her.

I got up to return to the hotel, hoping to find a cup of coffee. Crossing the beach, I looked up toward Messa Vouno. I could literally see the top section where Sara and I sat. I will never forget hearing the word "cancer" escape from her lips. It still screamed in my mind and I could still feel the chills in my spine.

I entered the hotel courtyard. The large coffee pot was still brewing. Barbara and Anna were busy inside preparing the daily buffet. No one else was in the area. Being a bit impatient, I put a mug under the pot and drew a few ounces of the brew. It looked dark enough, so I filled my cup and walked to the edge of the courtyard. I sat staring at the sea, pumping caffeine into my system.

I suddenly felt a hand on my shoulder. I turned my head sideways to see who was joining me. Sara gave me a soft kiss on the cheek.

"Good morning, sweetie," she said in a loving tone.

"Good morning, sweetie. Didn't expect you up so early."

"We leave in less than three hours. I wanted to enjoy it."

"Sit down. Let me get you a cup of coffee."

I immediately made my way over to the coffeepot as it had stopped brewing and the light indicated it was ready to serve. I also grabbed a glass of orange juice that had been set out for guests.

"Here you go, a little OJ and an infusion of caffeine."

"Thanks. I think I can use them both. How long have you been up?"

"Not too long. I walked around a bit waiting for the coffee."

"I'd like to take one more walk along the road before we leave."

"Sure thing."

Other guests were starting to make their way down for breakfast. Most exchanged morning greetings with some brief remarks, but coffee seemed to be the first thought on everyone's mind. Just as well, as Sara and I wanted to cherish the limited time we had left in Kamari.

Sara took her first sip of coffee. "Oh, that hits the spot. I think it needs to counteract a bit of lingering wine."

"I hear you."

"I was up a bit earlier this morning but just fooled around on my iPad. I was able to get the wifi," Sara said.

"Anything good?"

"I sent an email to Tommy and Kathy."

"What did you say?"

"Told them we get in at 3:00 p.m. on Sunday and invited them to dinner on Monday night."

"Do you think that's a good idea? Won't they think that you're trying to get into their business?"

"They didn't share anything with me, remember? As far as they know, I know nothing. Besides, I'm the mother and they're family. It will give them a chance to tell me."

"You're messing with fire."

"Not really. If they're going to counseling, they must be willing to talk. Maybe it will be easier for them to talk with me."

"You're the good listener. I know they're comfortable with you. Hope it goes well."

"I'm confident it'll be fine. I'm not saying that it'll help, but we can talk."

"Are you going to share your news?"

"No. I had an email confirming my doctor's appointment on Tuesday, so I really won't have all the facts. No need worrying them until we know more."

"I guess one thing at a time. What time is your appointment on Tuesday?"

"Tell you what, let's take a short walk. We can grab some more breakfast in a few minutes."

Sara stood up. I looked at her puzzled and concerned. She had abruptly suggested we take a walk and I was totally aware that she hadn't answered my question. Without hesitation, she pushed in her chair and extended her hand to me, as if to lead me away. I aimlessly put up my hand for her to grasp and followed her lead. It was an uneasy feeling, like being led out onto the dance floor by a high school date—awkward to say the least, but unfortunately the uneasy feeling indicated that my question had triggered a need for further discussion.

"Take a look around, we have to leave this wonderful place."

"I know," I said, feeling that my response was only filling in a gap of time.

"Let's walk over to the lounge chair where we sat last night."

"Okay," I said, not indicating that I'd been there earlier, but I was bewildered and uncertain of her purpose for this short side excursion.

Sara walked with a carefree motion. Her arms swung loosely at her side and her shoulders swayed. Her body communicated a relaxed feeling, which was the opposite of my rigid limbs. She seemed to purposely venture three to five yards in front of me with her lackadaisical waltz, as if she wanted to limit our conversation until we reached the lounger. I followed, expecting that we would communicate when we sat down.

"Here we are," she exclaimed. "Back at our spot."

"Yep, great spot," I said, sitting next to her.

"Just listen. I want to listen to the waves and the pebbles. Heavenly."

We sat quietly. Sara took a deep breath and closed her eyes. She truly enjoyed the unique sound of the waves on Kamari Beach. Though they were like no other waves I'd ever heard before, they currently were being drowned out by my thoughts. I knew Sara well and the waves were only part of the reason we were here.

Sara inhaled, exhaled and then opened her eyes. She broke the silence. "My appointment is at 10:00 a.m. on Tuesday."

"Oh, not too early," I responded, but still feeling like more information would come my way.

"The email I got this morning said I have the appointment with my doctor and that I have an appointment with a specialist on Wednesday."

"A specialist, before they even let you know what's going on."

"Everyone at my doctor's office has been good and very supportive. They encouraged me to take this vacation. In fact, they said it would take a couple of weeks to get the results of all the tests together. I really only delayed things a few days."

"Why the specialist?"

"It's not good, Jay. They must want to get me in right away. I'm really concerned the cancer has spread."

"Oh, Sara." The words barely made it out of my mouth.

I embraced her much the way I had last night. We swayed together, trying to comfort each other. Holding back tears and wanting to be strong I asked, "What's next?"

She looked at me. Her eyes reddened, but putting up a display of strength she calmly said, "I'm not sure. They told me there's an array of treatments. They won't tell me anything specific by email."

"Did they tell you anything?"

"Jay, I pretty much told you all I know. I have a tumor about two centimeters. It's cancer. I have to deal with it. What I haven't really shared is that on this trip I've had continual pain under my arm. That's why I think it may be in my lymph nodes."

"Oh honey, you don't know for sure."

"I know, but I feel my body is telling me something."

"I can't believe you've been dealing with all this by yourself."

"You've helped. This trip has been the best thing to keep my mind off things. It's been good. I'm living my dream."

"It's reality that's a bite in the ass."

"Only part, we made this trip reality. We jumped ship and I'll never regret it. I'll keep this spot close to me. It'll help me get through whatever has to happen."

I smiled at her positive twist on reality. She'd always been a strong woman and something told me that I hadn't yet seen her true strength.

"I don't want to keep badgering you about the next steps since you're really not sure, but be honest with me about what the doctors say and what I can do to help."

"I will. I've looked at the Internet a million times. It provides information and offers hope, but it scares me. I don't know what to expect. I just need to wait until I see my doctors."

"I've looked at the websites over the last couple of days too. I'm worried."

"You! It honestly scares the hell out of me. There were nights earlier on this trip that I laid awake at night in fear, but for whatever reason, leaving here, I feel like I'm ready."

"I guess, as ready as you can be."

"Really, I'm more at peace with my situation. My body isn't as stressed. I sense that I'll have to put up with a lot of unpleasant things and pain, but my body is more prepared."

"I admire you—more than ever."

She smiled. "I feel closer to you, more than ever. After thirty-five years together, I think I learned even more about you on this trip."

"Amidst everything else, I guess we took that time to talk and connect."

Adding a bit of humor, Sara laughed, "It was perfect."

I laughed, but she added, "It was perfect, really. It helped prepare me for the fight that I have in front of me. It only solidified my relationship with you. It emphasized to me that I need to live for the moment."

"Honestly, I'd be hard pressed to say it was perfect. Much of the time I struggled with the separation of the kids and the dilemma of telling you. The last couple of days have shredded my guts thinking about you."

"Jay," Sara said, stopping me from saying more. "We're going to go down a tough path together...together! If we have anything, we have a strong relationship. Do you realize how important it is to me to know that you're going to be there with me?"

I reached over to embrace her. I kissed her forehead and held her tight. Kamari had been a location where I was forced to deal with some difficult situations in life, yet I sensed I was leaving as a stronger person. I knew I'd have to deal with my fears of Sara's cancer and I knew I'd need to be strong for her.

Sara looked at me. "It's already after eight o'clock, we'd better grab a bite to eat and finish packing."

I nodded. We stood up and with my arm around Sara's shoulder, we listened to our waves. We walked back toward the hotel holding hands and occasionally glancing back at the beach.

Nearing the road, Sara paused. She pointed towards Messa Vouno.

"We climbed that rock," I said, but hating the thought it evoked.

"I'm going to use that rock to help me!"

"How?"

"To fight cancer. I read that you need to visualize beating cancer. In my mind, the steep cliffs will keep the cancer from reaching me. I'll seek shelter in the chapel for safety and pray for recovery. I'm going to be bold and as solid as Messa Vouno."

"That gives me a different image of that rock. I have no doubt you'll be solid—indestructible."

"I will be," said Sara firmly, as she started across the road for breakfast.

There was a determined look in her eyes and the posture of her walk was strong and erect. She seemed to be preparing herself for the reality of returning home. She didn't know the details, but she sensed she had a long fight ahead of her. I sensed this escape had prepared her for that fight.

As we entered the hotel courtyard, we were greeted warmly by the other guests. They'd been bantering with poor Diane about being in her Fifties, but in a good-natured way. Sara received a few compliments on her dancing while Spyros told me that he'd get his oil can out for my rusty joints at the next party. Good fun was had by all and the last couple of hours passed quickly.

Sara ran up to the room to put the few last things into her backpack. I cleared our table of the empty plates and cups. Since I was near the office, I stopped in and paid Diane for our stay. I sincerely thanked her for all their hospitality and expressed what a wonderful time we had at her birthday party.

I felt a bit depressed going up the stairs to our room. It was that dreary reality that our vacation was over, magnified by the issues that were waiting to be addressed when we got home. I wasn't looking forward to the long haul flight. My feet seemed heavy as I reached the top.

Sara was zipping her backpack shut as I entered our room. "I think I have everything. I checked under the bed, in the drawers and the safe. You have some bathroom items to collect."

"Yup. I'll brush my teeth and put my shaving kit in my suitcase and then I'll be ready."

"If you'd carry the packs down, I just want to make sure I say goodbye to Diane," said Sara moving toward the door.

I yelled in her direction, "I already paid the hotel bill."

She paused and looked back. "Did you leave a tip for the housekeepers and the girls at the bar?"

"Yup. Twenty euros each."

"Great!" she shouted, heading down the steps.

I collected the last of my things. I grabbed both packs and stood in the doorway. The balcony doors were open and I could see out to the sea. I took one last look out over the balcony. The breeze blowing in through the open doors seemed to let me know it was time to leave. I thumped down the stairs with both backpacks.

A smiling Spyros was waiting at the bottom of the stairs. "I'll throw those in the car for you."

I thanked him and walked across the courtyard. I hugged and shook hands with every person around the tables. In a short time we had developed such great relationships with all the other guests. The Boathouse had exceeded our expectations and offered us much more than just a place to sleep.

I hugged Teresa near the bar and shook hands with her husband, Brian. Evie was tending to her bar duties. "Has it been a week already?"

"It has...and thanks for everything. It'll be a week to remember."

Though I'm sure she knew that we'd enjoyed our week at the Boathouse, she fully didn't understand my response. In fact, I'm not sure how I'll look back on this vacation. In many ways it was a trip of a lifetime and in other ways it was a trip that changed our lives in an unexpected way.

Sara was now standing next to me. The moment had come and it was time to leave. We hugged Evie and started towards Spyros who was standing near the car.

Sara followed Spyros around the car to the driver's side. He opened the door and she climbed in the back. I hopped in the front passenger seat. Spyros started the car, which seemed to be the final signal ending our time on Santorini.

As I glanced back to an array of waving hands in the courtyard, I saw Diane running toward the car as if we had forgotten something. Spyros stopped the car and I rolled down the window.

Holding a piece of paper in her hand, Diane said, "Here's your receipt."

Looking confused I replied, "You already gave me my receipt."

"No, this is the one for next year's reservation that Sara made."

I started to respond, but Sara leaned forward and interrupted me. "Thanks, Diane! I'm already counting the days."

I took the paper from Diane and turned to hand it back to Sara. She was sitting there with smirk on her face. With a twinkle in her eyes, she exclaimed, "This woman has to have something to look forward to."

I handed her the receipt and smiled. There was a brief moment when our eyes met. It was as if we exchanged reassuring messages without saying a word. Spyros put the car in gear and I turned to face forward. Our Santorini escape was ending, but I knew our journey was just beginning. The road back to Santorini would present more obstacles than simply leaving a cruise ship.

As Spyros turned the corner and headed away from the village, I turned to look out the back window, attempting to get one last look at our spot on the beach. Instead I saw Sara looking straight forward with apparently no desire to look back. She looked directly at me and said, "Don't worry. we'll be back."

Greek Glossary

Ancient Thira	Archaeological site on top of Messa Vouno on the Island of Santorini. The ancient city was inhabited in 9th century BC by Doric colonists from Sparta.
Assyrtiko	Type of Greek white grape first cultivated on the Island of Santorini. It has the ability to maintain its acidity as it ripens.
Balos	Greek folk island dance specific to Santorini. It has a joyous and lyrical melody.
Baklava	Desert made from phyllo pastry filled with chopped nuts and soaked in honey.
Blue Flag	Designation for European beaches to show that they have a high standard of water quality, safety, services and environmental qualities.
Bouzouki	Greek string musical instrument. It has a metallic sound similar to a mandolin. The front is flat and the back side is rounded. It either has three or four pairs of strings.
Caldera	A large volcano crater formed by a major eruption leading to the collapse of the center of the volcano.
Dolmades or Dolmathes	Grape leaf stuffed with a mix of rice and fresh herbs, often garnished with lemon or yogurt.
Efharisto	Greek word for "Thank you".
Euro	Currency for the European Union, which is the currency for Greece.
Fava	1. Plant that produces the broad bean, which is a flat edible seed used in Greek recipes. 2. Greek appetizer or dip.
Fira	Santorini capital city located on the western side of the Island. It is known for its views from the caldera.
Imerovigli	City on Santorini that is adjacent to Fira.
Kalimera	Greek term for "Good Morning."

Kalispera	Greek term for "Good Afternoon" or "Good Evening."
Kamari	Coastal village on the southeastern side of Santorini. It is known for its long black sand beach.
Messa Vouno	Mountain between Kamari and Perissa that has steep, sheer rock sides.
Moussaka	Traditional Greek eggplant based casserole dish that is layered with an egg custard top layer.
Mykonos	Greek island which is a popular cruise port and known for its party atmosphere.
Nisiotika	Traditional folk dance of Greek islands.
Oia	Village on the northwestern tip of Santorini, known for its sunsets.
Ouzo	Greek anise flavored alcoholic drink
Parthenon	Preserved ancient temple in Athens dedicated to the goddess Athena. It is a popular tourist attraction.
Patmos	Small Greek island known for its connection to the Book of Revelation in the Bible.
Perissa	Village located on the east coast of Santorini. It has the longest beach on the island.
Pyrgos	Highest village on the island of Santorini.
Raki	Distilled, unsweetened alcoholic drink popular in Greece made from grape stems and seeds.
Rhodes	Greek island just off the Anatolian coast of Turkey. Popular destination for European tourists.
Souvlaki	Greek fast food that is grilled meat served on a skewer and often served in a pita sandwich.
Yamas	Greek term for "Cheers!" as in raising a glass for a toast.

About the Author

Jim LaBuda, Ed.D.

Jim is a lover of life and travel. He enjoys nothing more than slinging a backpack over his shoulder and setting off across the globe with his wife, Susan. He believes that travel is more about the people you meet along the way and less about the sites on your itinerary. Professionally, he was a nationally recognized educator. However, these days he prefers the title "Professional Beach Bum."

Leaving education behind and now following his dreams, Jim is a regular contributor to Destinations Travel Magazine and currently writes a travel column, "Side Roads". Jim's new adventure is never more than an airline ticket away.

Jim LaBuda